Overcoming Barriers to **Employment Success**

The Key to Getting and Keeping a Job

Second Edition

John J. Liptak, Ed.D.

CAREER SOLUTIONS
JIST

St. Paul

Director of Editorial: Christine Hurney
Director of Production: Tim Larson
Associate Production Editor: Eric Braem
Design and Production Specialist: Sara Schmidt Boldon
JIST Product Manager: Selena Hicks

Care has been taken to verify the accuracy of information presented in this book. However, the authors, editors, and publisher cannot accept responsibility for Web, e-mail, newsgroup, or chat room subject matter or content, or for consequences from application of the information in this book, and make no warranty, expressed or implied, with respect to its content.

Trademarks: Some of the product names and company names included in this book have been used for identification purposes only and may be trademarks or registered trade names of their respective manufacturers and sellers. The authors, editors, and publisher disclaim any affiliation, association, or connection with, or sponsorship or endorsement by, such owners.

Photo Credits: Cover photos (clockwise from upper left), © iStock.com/kali9, © iStock.com/IS_ImageSource, © iStock.com/laflor, © iStock.com/IS_ImageSource; **Cover background**, © iStock.com/RomanOkopny; **16**, © iStock.com/michaeljung; **36**, © iStock.com/BartCo; **55**, © iStock.com/asiseeit; **80**, © Stephen Coburn/Shutterstock.com; **97**, © wavebreakmedia/Shutterstock.com

We have made every effort to trace the ownership of all copyrighted material and to secure permission from copyright holders. In the event of any question arising as to the use of any material, we will be pleased to make the necessary corrections in future printings. Thanks are due to the aforementioned authors, publishers, and agents for permission to use the materials indicated.

ISBN 978-1-63332-030-7 (print)
ISBN 978-1-63332-040-6 (digital)

© 2015 by JIST Publishing, Inc.
875 Montreal Way
St. Paul, MN 55102
Email: info@jist.com
Website: http://JIST.com

The *Overcoming Barriers to Employment Success, Second Edition Instructor's Guide* is available for free download from http://jist.emcp.com/overcoming-barriers-2e.html. It contains chapter overviews with activities, discussion questions, and homework assignments. Also visit our website to find out more about our products, get free tables of contents and sample pages, order a catalog, and link to other career-related sites.

Please visit http://JIST.com for a free catalog and more information.

Printed in the United States of America

23 22 21 20 19 18 17 16   3 4 5 6 7 8 9 10

Contents

Introduction: Breaking Through

If you are reading this book, odds are you are looking for a job. Or maybe you are just looking to get ahead in one. Essentially, you are looking to make yourself more employable. The good news: This workbook can help you.

Employability is the ability to find a job, keep a job, and get a new job if the need should arise. But it's more than that. Employability is *your* ability to realize your full potential. It's your ability to meet your needs and the needs of your family. It's your ability to find success though your career.

Being employable means overcoming your barriers. People face employment barriers every day. A lack of money or transportation, insufficient education or training, a physical or mental disability, a lack of energy or low self-esteem, a lack of knowledge about how to even *find* a job—these are just some of the obstacles people just like you have to deal with.

Some of these barriers may be the result of your own actions. Some may be the work of outside forces. But all of the barriers that you have, or think you have, can be overcome. I have spent most of my professional career working with long-term unemployed people, including welfare-to-work clients, ex-offenders, and people who struggled for months to find a job. Nearly everyone I counseled faced multiple barriers. And they all found ways to overcome them.

You can do the same. This workbook is designed to help you identify your barriers, explore information that can help you to reduce or eliminate the barriers that are keeping you from being successfully employed, and begin to formulate an action plan. You are encouraged to work through each of the self-help sections. These sections are designed to help you reflect on your career, discover what may be contributing to your barriers to employment success, and think about ways to overcome and eliminate these barriers.

To solidify your action plan, consider completing the *Barriers to Employment Success Inventory (BESI)*. The inventory is available in both print and electronic formats from JIST Publishing, Inc., at http://JIST.com.

So turn the page, and don't let anything stand in your way.

PART 1

Personal and Financial Barriers

Success doesn't come easily to most people; many barriers stand in the way. Overcoming these barriers is the key to getting a good job and advancing your career. The good news is that all barriers can be overcome with support, knowledge, and hard work.

Personal and financial barriers are no exception. Such barriers arise from a lack of basic resources. People facing such barriers are most concerned about supporting themselves and their families while they look for work. This first chapter will help you to explore your personal and financial barriers and develop a plan to overcome them.

Personal Barriers

Can you look for a job without a car? Fill out an application without a permanent address? Find a sitter for your children while you go to an interview? Before you can conduct an effective job search, you need overcome your personal barriers. That means being able to fulfill your basic needs.

The following checklist will help you to identify the specific barriers you face in meeting your basic needs. Keep in mind that meeting these needs is a necessary first step toward finding employment. Which of these barriers are keeping you from finding or keeping a job?

- ☐ I need food to feed my family.
- ☐ I don't own a car.
- ☐ I don't have access to public transportation.
- ☐ I don't have clothes suitable for a job interview.
- ☐ I have a health problem that keeps me from working.
- ☐ I don't have a place to live.
- ☐ I don't have a mailing address.
- ☐ The place where I live is unsafe.
- ☐ I have dependents that need child care.
- ☐ I have children with special needs.

☐ I have family members with health problems requiring my care.

☐ I don't know whom to turn to for help.

☐ I don't know how to get government assistance.

☐ I have a criminal record.

☐ I am not a legal citizen.

☐ I am a displaced homemaker.

☐ I lack medical and dental benefits.

Some barriers will have more of an impact on your job search and success than others. Try to prioritize your barriers from most to least important. Use the barriers you checked above as your starting point, and then write your three most pressing basic needs.

_____

_____

_____

The following sections provide strategies and exercises for overcoming the most common barriers people face when meeting their basic needs.

Food and Clothing

Feeding yourself and your family is, obviously, a top priority. Thankfully there are government programs available to help you, including the following:

- **Women, Infants, and Children (WIC):** The US Department of Agriculture provides specific items such as milk, cheese, juice, eggs, infant formula, and other foods to WIC participants. WIC programs also include clinical screening and nutritional education for participants. You can apply for WIC benefits at http://www.fns.usda.gov/wic.

- **Supplemental Nutrition Assistance Program (SNAP) benefits:** The US Department of Agriculture sponsors a SNAP benefits program in each individual state. In these programs, people receive coupons redeemable at grocery stores, convenience stores, farmers' markets, and restaurants. The amount received is often dependent upon family size and income. You can apply for SNAP benefits at http://www.fns.usda.gov/snap.

- **Temporary Assistance for Needy Families (TANF):** TANF helps you maintain your family until you become self-sufficient and self-supporting. The program is administered by the US Department of Health and Human Services, found online at http://acf.hhs.gov/programs/ofa/help.

- **Food banks:** Many food banks are available that will provide food to you and your family. To find a food bank near you, go to http://feedingamerica.org.

It's also important to cut down on food expenses whenever possible. Avoid eating out often, as the food is more expensive and less nutritious than what you would make at home. Be sure to save leftovers and learn to make meals that will keep well. Most importantly, be a smart shopper: Look carefully at grocery ads and use coupons whenever possible.

> Take a grocery list with you when you shop and stick to it. This will help you avoid buying things you don't really need.

The same is true for clothing. You will need professional attire for interviewing, but you should shop around. Goodwill stores carry clothing of all kinds at affordable prices—including dress clothes suitable for interviewing. Check anything you buy for tears, holes, stains, missing buttons, and the like.

List the steps you can take to get the food and clothing you need. _____

_____

_____

_____

Housing

Do you have a place to live? Is it a place you can afford? Is it safe, clean, and comfortable? Is it in need of major repairs? Does it meet the needs of yourself and your family? Having adequate housing is just as important as having enough food. Your living situation should not only be clean and safe, it should also be a good place to conduct a job search from. That means having a space to work, phone service, and, if possible, an Internet connection (though the latter can be expensive and isn't necessary provided you can get access elsewhere).

There are a variety of housing options available, and many government agencies can help you find a place to live. The following lists a few of the possibilities available to you:

- **Renting a house or apartment:** Renting is a good solution to your housing problems, especially if you are able to find a rental that is near a bus or subway station or is close to work or potential employers.

- **Buying a house:** With government incentive programs, such as the Low-Income Housing Tax Credit program, you might be able to purchase your own home.

- **Habitat for Humanity:** Volunteers at Habitat for Humanity build and rehabilitate simple, decent houses with the help of the homeowner family. This is not a giveaway program; in addition to the down payment and monthly mortgage payments, homeowners invest hundreds of hours of their own labor in building their house. Families in need of housing can apply at their local Habitat for Humanity office.

- **Living with family/friends:** This is a good but temporary solution to your housing problems. You should consider this option as a stopgap until you find a permanent solution.

- **Section 8 housing:** This is permanent housing that is subsidized by the federal government for very low-income families, the elderly, and the disabled. Rent is based on your income. This program is operated by the US Department of Housing and Urban Development (HUD).

- **Shelters:** Shelters, such as those offered by the Salvation Army, offer you overnight or very short-term housing, usually no more than thirty days. You should think of this as a way to address emergency needs, but not as a long-term solution.

While resources will vary from city to city, there are probably a number of organizations and government agencies in your area that can help you find a place to live. The following are good places to start:

- Habitat for Humanity (http://habitat.org)

- Low-income and subsidized housing finder (http://findaffordablehousing.org)

- National Coalition for the Homeless (http://nationalhomeless.org)

- Resources to help with bills, mortgages, and debt (http://needhelppayingbills.com)

- Salvation Army (http://salvationarmy.org)

- US Department of Housing and Urban Development (http://hud.gov)

- Volunteers of America at (http://voa.org)

List the steps you can take to find a place to live or to improve your housing situation.

_____

_____

_____

_____

Transportation

Most employers assume that their employees have ways to get to work. Whether it's a car, the city bus system, or a subway, you will need a reliable and affordable way to look for a job or get to work. You won't make a good first impression if you show up late to an interview because you didn't know the bus schedule or because your car broke down.

The following lists some of the transportation options that might be available to you. Keep in mind that not all cities or towns have reliable public transportation:

- **Public transportation:** Many cities have a bus, train, or subway system. If your public transportation system offers a monthly or yearly pass, it is usually cheaper than paying for each ride individually.

- **Your own automobile:** Owning your own vehicle is certainly the most convenient option. Just take the cost of upkeep (gas, maintenance, and insurance) into consideration. An unreliable car can be a barrier in itself.

- **Carpool:** Once you are hired, find someone you work with who lives close to you and volunteer to alternate who drives.

> Carpooling is a good way to save money on gas. Just make sure you can count on the people you are driving with.

- **Find work close to home:** On nice days it might be possible to walk or bike to work. Short commutes also save money on gas.

- **Friends and family:** Never be afraid to ask for help from those close to you.

List the steps you can take to get reliable transportation. Be sure to list any repairs you would need to make on your own automobile as well.

_____

_____

_____

_____

Family Concerns

Taking care of children or other family members is difficult enough without having to also find a job. Without the proper support, it can be impossible to find the time to conduct a job search. And of course, making sure your family is taken care of is always a top priority.

It can be especially difficult to search for a job while taking care of children at home. Child-care issues are one of the biggest barriers for people searching for a job. After all, most prospective employers don't appreciate you bringing your toddler to an interview.

> Some employers offer free or reduced-cost child-care services to employees. Think about this as you research and interview with companies you'd like to work for.

The key to overcoming such barriers is to create a support network and a child-care plan before beginning your job search. The following worksheet can help you develop such a plan.

■■□ My Child-Care Options

Identify child-care options that are available to you in order to determine which option best fits your needs.

Someone I Know and Trust

A family member who could watch my children while I look for work:

_____

A friend or neighbor who could watch my children while I look for work:

_____

How I could repay this person/people for helping me with child care:

_____

Low-Cost Child-Care Programs

Church-related programs: _____

_____

Community center/YWCA programs: _____

_____

WIC programs: _____

_____

Government-sponsored child-care programs in my community: _____

_____

_____

_____

_____

If you are taking care of others, such as sick family members or children with special needs, it is often difficult to put yourself first. However, if you don't take care of yourself, you won't be able to take care of anyone else. Following are some suggestions for taking care of yourself while you take care of others:

- **Prioritize your needs.** Be sure to schedule time out for you to look for a job, but also some time for you to relax, exercise, and engage in leisure interests.

- **Consider respite care.** Look into respite care that may be available to you at affordable prices. Medicaid may pay for home care while you search for employment if it is an elderly person you are caring for.

- **Get others involved.** Ask other family members, friends, or neighbors to care for the person while you conduct your job search.

- **Research programs that can help.** Many churches and synagogues have programs where members of the congregation will provide temporary in-home care, giving you the opportunity to find a job.

■■□ They're There to Help

There are a variety of agencies in the community that can assist you with employment problems. The following are common resources and organizations you can contact:

Agency	How They Can Help
Offices of Employment Security	They offer unemployment insurance benefits and job-search assistance. They also help enroll individuals in training and apprenticeship programs.
CareerOneStop programs (http://careeronestop.org)	They provide job seekers with a variety of services, including self-assessments, pay for educational and training programs, resume development advice, interview coaching, wage and salary information, relocation assistance, and information about occupations and employment trends.
Department of Social Services (DSS)	It provides services and financial support for low-income, aged, blind, and disabled adults and children. Services include cash assistance for immigrants, veteran's cash benefits programs, in-home support services, and the Supplemental Security Income (SSI) and State Supplemental Payment (SSP) programs.

Criminal Record

A criminal record can be a "red flag" for many employers. Even though you have served your time and are rehabilitated, employers may still question whether you are trustworthy, safe, and dependable.

Remember that many ex-offenders are able to find jobs and be successful. If you have been convicted of a crime in the past, you can take steps to overcome this barrier:

- **Be aware of the limitations of your conviction.** Apply for jobs for which you are qualified and which you can obtain. For example, people convicted of a felony usually cannot get jobs enforcing laws, working around prescription drugs, or handling money.

- **Don't lie.** Tell the truth when filling out an employment application or when answering interview questions. If you lie and an employer does a background check, you can be disqualified for the position.

- **Use cold calling to find a job.** By using this job-search method, you can avoid having your resume screened out before you get a chance to present your qualifications. For more on this, see Part 4.

- **Prepare your answers to difficult questions.** You may be asked "tough" questions about your conviction and incarceration in an employment interview. You should try and be honest and straightforward in answering questions, but do not go into too much detail. Stress that you take responsibility for what you did, you suffered the consequences, and you are now a changed person.

- **Make a good impression.** When hunting for a job, dress for success, maintain eye contact, stand up straight (which shows good self-esteem), and be direct and honest.

■■□ Resources for Ex-offenders

There are no federal programs exclusively for ex-offenders. Federal programs are generally designed to help people who need jobs, housing, public assistance, and other services. Each program has different standards for participation, but low income is the most common requirement. Most assistance programs for ex-offenders are administered locally by community agencies. You can find the addresses for them in the local telephone book's blue pages and on the Internet.

One of the first stops you should make for help with job leads is to a One-Stop Career Center. You can find their local addresses in the blue pages of the telephone book, online, or by calling their toll-free hotline: 1-877-US2-JOBS. You should ask the local CareerOneStop representatives about job-search assistance, federal bonding, employer tax incentives, job training, and Workforce Investment Act–sponsored training. The One-Stop Career Center will likely have information about community-assistance programs for ex-offenders.

Non-citizen Status

The US government is continuing to crack down on the number of immigrants entering the country illegally. If you are an illegal immigrant, you need to begin the process to become a legal resident. There are several ways you can do this:

- Apply for lawful permanent residence (LPR) or a Green Card. Green Cards give you official immigration status in the United States.

- Apply for a work visa. Various visas exist depending on your skills, education, profession, and country of origin.

- Find an employer who is willing to "sponsor" you while you complete the process of gaining legal status by completing a Petition for Alien Worker form.

- Apply for US citizenship. Be aware that there are several requirements for becoming a citizen.

For more information on these options, contact US Citizenship and Immigration Services at 1-800-375-5283 or at http://uscis.gov.

Make a Plan

Now that you have identified your most pressing personal barriers and read about some strategies for overcoming them, it is time to make a plan to do just that. Use the exercise that follows to help you decide on the next steps to take.

■■□ Getting Help for Basic Needs

In the left column, list the basic needs barriers that you are most concerned with. In the middle column, list creative and practical strategies for overcoming those barriers. In the right column, list the specific agencies in your community that can assist you with meeting that particular need.

My Basic-Needs Barrier	Strategies for Overcoming This Barrier	Agencies and Resources That Can Help
_____	_____	_____
_____	_____	_____
_____	_____	_____
_____	_____	_____
_____	_____	_____

Financial Barriers

Money is a problem for many people who are looking for a job. Trying to "make ends meet" while unemployed can be difficult. You may be so concerned with paying your next set of bills that it is hard to concentrate on your job search. To be successful, however, you will need to find ways to manage the money you do have until you land your next job.

The information that follows will help you think about your relationship with money: how much you spend, how much you save, and what you can do to overcome your financial hurdles.

> The average worker changes jobs 15 to 20 times in a lifetime. Temporary unemployment is a fact of life for just about everyone. It's not just you.

Managing Your Money

People approach money differently. Some hoard it, while others spend every last cent. Managing the money earned from work can be difficult. Money management requires careful planning, but it also requires a basic understanding of your options. Most importantly, it involves knowing when to spend, when to save, and how to do both wisely.

Whether you are employed or unemployed, you should put your money in the bank for safe keeping and to help you manage your money. A few good things about a bank are that it's a safe place to keep your money, you earn interest on any money you have in a saving's account, and you can move your money to and from checking accounts, savings accounts, certificates of deposit, savings bonds, and mutual funds. Let's take a look at each of these:

- **Checking account:** Regardless of how much money you actually have to save, you should still have a checking account. This will allow you to cash your paychecks easily or your employer to deposit them to you directly (electronically), without having to pay expensive check-cashing fees. A checking account also allows you to write checks to pay bills. Keeping a balanced checkbook is a good way to see whether you are staying within budget as well. Some banks offer free checking accounts, with or without a minimum balance, while others may charge a fee.

> Many employers will offer direct deposit of your paycheck into your checking or savings account. Not receiving a paper check can help reduce the temptation to spend your newly earned money.

- **Savings account:** Savings accounts allow you to save your money in a safe place while earning a small amount of interest. These accounts are insured so that there is limited risk involved.

- **Certificate of deposit (CD):** Certificates of deposit are purchased through a bank. They can be purchased to mature (earn their full amount of interest) in anywhere from one month to several years. These are safe investments that pay relatively low rates of return, usually around 1% to 2% annually.

- **Savings bond:** You can sign up for US savings bonds through payroll-deduction plans at work or you can purchase them directly from the US Treasury at http://treasurydirect.gov. Savings bonds make great long-term investments.
- **Mutual fund with stocks and bonds:** Another way to save your money is through a 401K/403B account, if you are employed, or an Individual Retirement Account (IRA). These types of accounts are designed for saving money for retirement. Keep in mind that if you choose to take money out of one of these accounts prior to retirement, you will incur a penalty. Therefore, any money you deposit into these accounts should be money that you will not need until after you retire. Remember, too, that although stocks may provide you with the best return on your money, they also have a certain amount of risk and their values are affected by swings in the economy.

Saving and Investing

Saving is holding on to money you have left over after paying your bills and putting it somewhere that you can earn interest and see the money grow. *Investing* is putting your money into a vehicle (such as a bond or a mutual fund) with the potential of earning much more (or losing it as well). Investing comes with greater potential rewards and more risk. Your plan for saving and investing your money often depends on the amount of risk you are willing to take.

Financial planners usually suggest that you begin saving by putting your money in a savings account in the bank and letting it grow. In a savings account, your money is insured by the US federal government. As your money begins to grow, you can then begin to invest it in other, potentially more rewarding, options.

Needs versus Wants

Before you can manage your money effectively, it is important to understand the differences between "needs" and "wants." *Needs* are those things that you must have for survival, such as food and shelter. *Wants*, on the other hand, are those things that you would like to have but could do without. Sometimes needs and wants overlap, but it is critical that you spend some time thinking about what your true needs and wants are, and then separate the two.

Making—and Sticking to—a Budget

It is important that you begin to figure out how much money you are spending each month and what you are spending it on. The following worksheet can help you determine your monthly expenses. From there you can begin to find ways to cut costs and save money.

■■□ My Monthly Budget

Monthly Expenses	Amount Paid	Monthly Expenses	Amount Paid
Living Expenses		**Insurance**	
Mortgage/rent	$_____	Health insurance	$_____
Electricity/gas	$_____	Auto insurance	$_____
Water	$_____	Homeowner's/renter's insurance	$_____
Telephone	$_____		
Television service	$_____	**Family Expenses**	
Internet service	$_____	Food (total grocery expenses—	
Sewage	$_____	not including eating out)	$_____
Sanitation	$_____	Clothes	$_____
Taxes	$_____	Child care	$_____
Household repairs/upkeep	$_____	Toys/games/activities	$_____
		Child support payments	$_____
Transportation Expenses		School tuition/supplies	$_____
Bus/train/taxi fare	$_____	Pet care	$_____
Vehicle payment/rental	$_____		
Gasoline	$_____	**Other Debt**	
Parking	$_____	Loan payments (other	
Vehicle repairs	$_____	than mortgage or car)	$_____
		Credit card interest	$_____
Entertainment Expenses			
Sporting events	$_____	**Miscellaneous Expenses**	
Movies	$_____	Higher education costs	
Eating out	$_____	(tuition, books, etc.)	$_____
Vacations	$_____	Newspaper/magazine/website	
Babysitters	$_____	subscriptions	$_____
Other entertainment	$_____	Club/association fees	$_____
Medical Expenses		**TOTAL MONTHLY EXPENSES**	$_____
Medical expenses	$_____		
Dental expenses	$_____	**TOTAL MONTHLY INCOME**	
		(include all sources of income from all contributing family members)	$_____

Look at the worksheet you just completed. If your total expenses are greater than your income, then you need to manage your money more carefully. That means knowing which expenses you can't change (your needs, such as food, electricity, water, and child care) and those you can (your wants, such as eating out or cable television).

Make a list of all of the *wants* you can do without. _____

_____

_____

_____

We are all tempted to spend money we don't have or to spend money we do have on things we shouldn't. Finding and keeping a good job means being financially stable and responsible, however. That often means finding ways to limit your spending, especially while you are unemployed.

While creating a budget is an excellent way to help limit your spending, there are other strategies. List some things you can do to limit your spending. Some suggestions might include cutting up your credit cards, seeing a financial planner, consolidating your loans, or canceling unnecessary services.

_____

_____

_____

▦▦▢ Debt: The Problem That Piles Up

One of the biggest financial barriers that many people in the United States face today is consumer debt, often in the form of credit card debt. In fact, nearly half of all Americans spend more than they earn each year. According to Janet Luhrs, author of *The Simple Living Guide,* there are several ways to reduce your debt:

- Get rid of all of your credit cards but one. The more cards you have, the more tempting it is to spend money you don't really have.

- Keep the credit card that has no annual fee and the lowest interest rate, but use it only in emergencies.

- Put off any purchasing decision for 24 hours and then think about whether you *need* to make the purchase or simply *want* to make the purchase.

- Do not purchase anything on any kind of installment plan until you have paid your debts in full.

Financial Barriers and the Job Search

Financial barriers can significantly impact your search for employment. Regardless of whether you need financial assistance for food, clothing, transportation, child care, or housing, the fact is that the longer you are unemployed, the more difficult it will be to pay for the necessities. Thus it is important that you identify which financial resources are most important for you at this point in time.

Complete the following worksheet by ranking your financial needs and then identifying how you will find financial resources for these needs.

■■□ My Financial Needs

In the middle column, identify your most pressing financial concerns by ranking them from one to seven, with one being your greatest concern. In the right-hand column, list steps you can take to meet your most important financial concerns.

Financial Concern	Ranking	How I Can Meet This Need
Transportation	_____	_____
Child Care	_____	_____
Medical/Dental Bills	_____	_____
Housing	_____	_____
Food	_____	_____
Clothes	_____	_____
Other _____	_____	_____

■■□ Working While You Look for Work

If you are looking for a full-time job, it can be tempting to ignore all part-time options. But you shouldn't. The demand for hourly and part-time employees has increased significantly with changes in the workplace. If money becomes a problem while you search for full-time employment, you may need to get a temporary job to sustain you and your family. Temporary jobs have many advantages. Temporary jobs

- give you something to do while you continue to look for full-time employment.

- help you to get into an organization so you are considered first if a full-time job opens up.

(continues)

- provide a source of income.
- allow you to meet new people who could be potential sources of job leads.
- allow you to gain experience, add to your work skills, and try out new occupations.
- provide you with much-needed self-confidence. Job-search experts say that it is easier to find a job when you already have one.

Such part-time work takes a variety of forms and is referred to by many names, including *contract work, odd jobs, seasonal work, freelance,* or *temporary (temp) jobs.* Examples of this type of work could include painting houses, walking dogs for people in the community, substitute teaching, or doing electrical work for a contractor.

You can look for temporary jobs through your state workforce agency, in classified ads, by talking to people in your network, or by going to a temporary staffing agency.

Planning Your Financial Future

It's never too early to plan for the future. Once you solve the short-term problem of a steady paycheck, you need to think about your long-term financial success. Are money and success the same for you? Do you have plans for moving up in the organization you're with? Do you want to go back to school and earn a degree? Do you hope to own a house, raise a family, or travel the world? Do you have plans for retirement?

Write down some long-term goals you have for your career and your life. Don't worry about whether you have the time or money to accomplish these goals now.

_____

_____

_____

Most of our long-term dreams are achievable, but not without careful money management. College is expensive. Saving for retirement takes time. Buying a home requires good credit. By carefully managing your money now, you not only knock down barriers to employment, you also build a sound financial future.

◼◼◻ Start Thinking about Retirement

If you are 25 or older, then it's time to start thinking about retirement. In order to retire comfortably at the age of 65, it is crucial to start saving as early as possible. As you look for jobs, be sure to ask each employer about their benefits packages. Ask about 401(k)s and profit sharing, and take advantage of the plans offered to you.

Summary

Personal and financial barriers are the most important to address if you are to be successful finding or keeping a job. Finding a place to live, money to support you and your family while you look for employment, people to care for your children, or transportation to get to job interviews can be overwhelming. It may seem impossible, but these barriers *can* be overcome. The key is to set priorities, understand your options, and, most importantly, be willing to ask for help.

▨▨▢ Barrier Breakers

Rania is a single mother who worked in a personnel office. She completed a year of college but had to drop out and make money to support her family. She struggled to get child support from her husband. She struggled to afford new shoes for her three-year-old son. She struggled just to make ends meet. Then, on top of it all, she was laid off from her last job.

Rania was unemployed for two months. Her money started to run out and she could no longer afford day care. She struggled to find time for job-hunting while watching her kids. Worst of all, she refused to ask for help. She had no support network in place and was too proud to admit that she couldn't make it on her own.

Finally, she decided to ask for assistance. She took advantage of her church's short-term, low-cost child-care program so that she could spend time finding job leads and going out on interviews. She went to the SNAP office to apply for a SNAP EBT card. She borrowed some dress clothes from a close friend to wear to interviews.

Most importantly, she devoted much more attention to her job search. With her kids in safe hands and a borrowed business suit, she hit the streets and quickly found a job in public relations. Though she can now afford full-time child care and her own dress clothes, she no longer minds asking for help when she needs it.

PART 2

Emotional and Physical Barriers

Are you frustrated because nobody will hire you? Do you feel depressed? Do you have health problems that prevent you from looking for work? If so, you may be suffering from emotional and physical barriers. These barriers to employment success are tricky because they can quickly get out of hand.

It is natural to get upset when you can't find or keep a job, but successful people are able to control their emotions and overcome their physical limitations. If you are experiencing emotional or physical barriers, this chapter can help you to cope with them. Even if some of what follows doesn't seem to apply to you now, you might still gain valuable information that you can use in the future.

Emotional Barriers

Emotional barriers include being unable to understand or control your emotions, being unable to stay positive in tough times, and being unable to cope with the pressures involved in the job search. Of course finding a job is stressful. However, when you find that these emotions interfere with your personal life or your job search, it's time to make some changes.

Take a moment to assess your current emotional state. On each the charts that follow, circle the number that describes where you stand on each scale:

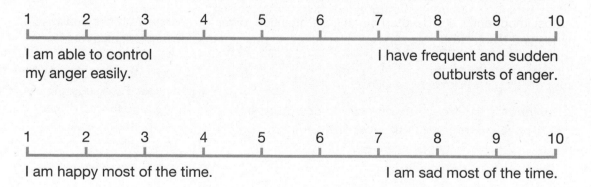

1	2	3	4	5	6	7	8	9	10

I am able to control
my anger easily.   I have frequent and sudden
                                                    outbursts of anger.

1	2	3	4	5	6	7	8	9	10

I am happy most of the time.   I am sad most of the time.

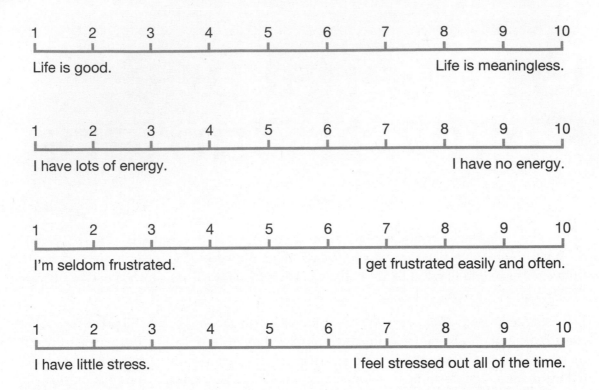

| 1 | 2 | 3 | 4 | 5 | 6 | 7 | 8 | 9 | 10 |

Life is good.   Life is meaningless.

I have lots of energy.   I have no energy.

I'm seldom frustrated.   I get frustrated easily and often.

I have little stress.   I feel stressed out all of the time.

These types of emotions are common. However, experiencing just one of these emotions at a high level (a score of 8 to 10) can have a dramatic impact on your physical and emotional well-being. That, in turn, will impact your job search or your job performance. The secret is to find tools and techniques to control these emotions. The information and exercises that follow can help you do just that.

> If you find yourself saying things like, "She made me mad," or, "He frustrates me," you are letting other people control how you feel. Remember that you, and you alone, control your full range of emotions.

Evaluating Your Support Network

The first step to overcoming emotional barriers is recognizing your need for help. Social support comes in the form of family, friends, and mentors and has a positive impact on your self-esteem. A lack of social support can be a major cause of stress and can act as a barrier in itself.

The following exercise can help you to determine how strong your support network is. From there you can discover ways to make that network stronger.

> Think of your support network as a team of people dedicated to helping you achieve your goals. By discussing your goals and dreams with others, you keep the ideas alive.

■■□ How Strong Is Your Network?

Read each of the statements and decide whether or not the statement describes you. If the statement *does* describe you, insert a check mark in the check box in the **True** column for that item. If the statement does *not* describe you, insert a check mark in the check box in the **False** column for that item.

	True	False
Sometimes I feel alone in the world.	☐ 1	☐ 2
I have lots of friends.	☐ 2	☐ 1
I rarely get invited out socially.	☐ 1	☐ 2
My friends and family are reliable.	☐ 2	☐ 1
I often feel unloved.	☐ 1	☐ 2
I think real friends are hard to find.	☐ 1	☐ 2
I get moral support from others.	☐ 2	☐ 1
My family lives too far away.	☐ 1	☐ 2
The people in my life make me feel good about myself.	☐ 2	☐ 1
I have at least one mentor.	☐ 2	☐ 1
I have a set of core friends I can count on.	☐ 2	☐ 1
I find it difficult to ask others for help.	☐ 1	☐ 2
I'm surrounded by negative people.	☐ 1	☐ 2
I rarely get to share ideas with others.	☐ 1	☐ 2
I have people I can talk to about my problems.	☐ 2	☐ 1
I see a professional counselor to help me deal with problems.	☐ 2	☐ 1
The people in my life don't respect me.	☐ 1	☐ 2
I have people around who encourage me.	☐ 2	☐ 1
My friends rarely do things to help me.	☐ 1	☐ 2
I have people I can go to for advice.	☐ 2	☐ 1

Add the scores you placed check marks next to above to get your Support Network Total. Write that number in the space below.

Support Network Total = _____

You should get a score between 20 and 40. Scores from **34 to 40** are **high** and indicate that you have a lot of people in your support network who can help you achieve your goals and overcome barriers to employment success. Scores from **27 to 33** are **average**, indicating that you have some people in your support network who can help you achieve your goals and overcome barriers to employment success. Scores from **20 to 26** are **low** and indicate that you only have a few people in your network who can help you achieve your goals. A lack of a support network may be acting as a barrier to your employment success.

Developing Your Support System

Success does not occur in a vacuum. Rarely can you do everything alone. In most cases, you must work with other people to meet your goals. Without the support of others, you won't stay motivated.

You will need to share your employment goals with family, friends, and colleagues. You must begin to think of yourself as part of a team. Start by identifying the people in your life who can help you. These should be people to whom you can turn to help you get your life together, find a job, or get ahead. You need people who will encourage you if you begin to lose your motivation. Following are just some of the kinds of people that are typically included in a support system:

- **Role models:** *Role models* are people you would like to pattern your life after. They represent qualities or characteristics that you would like to have. Role models can be friends, athletes, entertainers, family members, or people in your community. List the names of role models you would like to be part of your support network.

  _____

  _____

- **Mentors:** Most successful people have mentors. *Mentors* are people who serve as guides and advisers to you as you work to fulfill your dreams. They can provide you with inspiration, information, direction, and support. Mentors might be teachers, coworkers, friends, relatives, community leaders, significant others, or clergy members. List the names of people who might be potential mentors to you.

  _____

  _____

- **Significant others:** *Significant others* are your closest friends and family. They are the people you trust the most. They are the people who know your strengths and weaknesses and thus are often in the best position to offer constructive criticism. They should be reliable, encouraging, and interested in your well-being. List the names of your significant others.

  _____

  _____

Now use the worksheet that follows to list the people who you think will support you. Remember, they might be family members, friends, colleagues, or professionals (such as job coaches or counselors). Consider what kind of support you need from each person. Examples of the types of support you might need include emotional support, practical help (such as a ride to an interview), advice, instruction, and encouragement.

■■□ My Support Network

People Who Will Support Me

_____

_____

_____

_____

_____

_____

_____

_____

_____

What I Need from Them

_____

_____

_____

_____

_____

_____

_____

_____

_____

Taking Responsibility

To overcome emotional roadblocks to employment success, you must first accept responsibility for your actions and your career. By accepting responsibility, you are able to take greater control of your life.

People who struggle to get or keep jobs often fall into old habits. They blame their lack of success on others, complain about their bad luck, or make excuses for themselves. This often leads to the same, ineffective behaviors and ultimately to a lack of action.

You are ultimately responsible for everything that happens in your life—the good and the bad. You are responsible for your past, present, and future. You may find yourself in tough situations with difficult choices, but it is how you react to those situations that matters most. Losing a job is difficult. So is looking for work. But both of these are also opportunities, and you have the power to make the most of them.

Some people may feel threatened by your efforts to find a job or improve your situation. Be selective when building your support network. Find the people who believe in you and whom you can count on. Ignore people who tell you what you *can't* do.

◼◼◻ Responsibility or Blame?

Taking responsibility is not the same as blaming yourself. Often when things go wrong, people feel that if they had just done something differently, everything would have turned out all right. Ultimately, this attitude can be self-defeating.

People who constantly criticize themselves often suffer from low self-esteem. Because they feel unable to make the right choices, they refuse to take any action at all. While such people *are* taking the blame, they are *not* taking any responsibility for improving their situations. Don't blame yourself for every problem. Just take responsibility for how you handle them.

The exercise that follows can help you think about ways you can take more responsibility for your actions. As you complete the worksheet, be sure to focus on *you* (instead of others) and on the *present* (instead of the past). What can you do to take more responsibility and change your life?

◼◼◻ Taking Responsibility

Complete the following sentences.

1. I will take responsibility for my actions by _____

    _____

    _____

    _____

2. I will take responsibility for my family by _____

    _____

    _____

    _____

3. I will take responsibility for my education by _____

    _____

    _____

    _____

(continues)

4. I will take responsibility for my career by _____

_____

_____

_____

Maintaining Your Self-Esteem

Self-esteem is your perception of your worth. This self-image is a combination of your personal appearance, skills, abilities, intelligence, personality, and status. Positive self-esteem is essential to career success. You must *believe* that you can take control of your career and find the job that you want.

> "Each player must accept the cards life deals him or her: but once they are in hand, he or she alone must decide how to play the cards in order to win the game." —Voltaire

Self-esteem can be linked to success in school, in relationships, and at work. If you haven't had much success in finding work, you may struggle with low self-esteem. Your self-esteem has a direct impact on how capable you feel and how confident you are to face life's problems.

Negative self-esteem can lead to feelings of helplessness. When you have low self-esteem, you take fewer risks and have less motivation. That makes it difficult to network for a job, interview with a potential employer, or even get up and go to work.

■■□ Success and Self-Esteem

We all gain confidence as we experience success. This, in turn, increases our self-esteem. Winners tend to focus on successes and put failures behind them. Losers, on the other hand, focus on their failures and forget past successes.

One secret to employment and career success is to engage in those activities at which you are successful. Use the space below to list five things that you do well. They do not necessarily have to be work related. These things should be sources of pride for you.

Things That I Do Well

1. _____

2. _____

3. _____

4. _____

5. _____

Emotional and Physical Barriers

Maintaining self-esteem is an acquired skill, much like tying your shoes. You can heal your self-esteem by changing the ways you view yourself. People with high self-esteem recognize their strengths but also accept their limitations and continually try to grow and improve.

The following exercise can help you think positively by changing the way you see yourself and the world around you.

Making Lemonade

All people have things they like about themselves and things they don't. You are no different. This is the perfect opportunity for you to make lemonade out of lemons. You have the power to change things about yourself if you want to.

The first step is to identify the things that you would like to change about yourself or your situation. Then, visualize a positive outcome of the change and make a plan to create the change in yourself. Use the spaces below to get started. An example is provided.

What I Want to Change About Myself or My Situation	A Positive Outcome of This Change	How I Will Make This Change
I don't want to be angry all the time.	I will be a more patient and forgiving person.	I need to learn anger management skills.

Managing Stress

For most of us, life is stressful, and unemployment is especially so. While a little bit of stress can help you to meet challenges, too much stress can hurt your ability to succeed. Research shows that the stress of unemployment can lead to depression, headaches, alcoholism, and even suicide. Take a moment to assess your current stress level using the following exercise.

◼◼◻ How Stressed Are You?

Read each of the statements and decide whether or not the statement describes you. If the statement *does* describe you, insert a check mark in the check box in the **True** column for that item. If the statement does *not* describe you, insert a check mark in the check box in the **False** column for that item.

	True	False
I often have trouble thinking clearly.	☐ 2	☐ 1
I like being around other people.	☐ 1	☐ 2
I find myself forgetting things lately.	☐ 2	☐ 1
I often have a strong urge to "run away from things."	☐ 2	☐ 1
I am eager to get up in the mornings.	☐ 1	☐ 2
I often cry unexpectedly.	☐ 2	☐ 1
I rarely have emotional ups and downs.	☐ 1	☐ 2
I am rarely nervous.	☐ 1	☐ 2
I am often afraid of what's going to happen next.	☐ 2	☐ 1
I rarely get depressed.	☐ 1	☐ 2
I feel as if I have little control over my life.	☐ 2	☐ 1
I rarely lash out at other people.	☐ 1	☐ 2
I often feel short-tempered.	☐ 2	☐ 1
I usually get at least seven hours of sleep a night.	☐ 1	☐ 2
I think before acting.	☐ 1	☐ 2
I have a healthy appetite.	☐ 1	☐ 2
I feel tired a lot of the time.	☐ 2	☐ 1
I have experienced chest pain in the last six months.	☐ 2	☐ 1
I often have an upset stomach.	☐ 2	☐ 1
I get headaches often.	☐ 1	☐ 2

Add the scores you placed check marks next to above to get your Stress Total. Write that number in the space below.

Stress Total = _____

A high score (33 or more) on the exercise you just completed indicates that you are probably experiencing a great deal of stress and should take steps to manage it. Try doing all of the stress-management techniques listed on the following page and then plan on repeating the ones you feel most comfortable doing:

- **Deep breathing:** When you encounter stressful situations, your breathing quickens and becomes shallower. Taking long, very deep breaths can help you to relax. Take a moment to draw in a long deep breath; then exhale as slowly and as long as possible. How do you feel?

- **Exercising:** Exercise is an excellent way to combat stress. Though it can be hard to find the time and energy, it is important to exercise weekly—daily, if possible. Exercise not only helps to relieve stress, it will also boost your energy level. This can be important during the exhaustive process of searching for a job.

- **Listening to music:** Studies have shown that listening to music can help people to relax and reduce stress. Select music that you find peaceful. Try to set aside 20 to 30 minutes of uninterrupted listening time daily.

- **Meditating:** Meditation is the practice of focusing your attention on one thing at a time. You use repeated mental focus to quiet your mind, which in turn quiets your body. Consider meditating for at least 15 minutes a day to help clear your mind and relax your body.

- **Eating right:** People often eat more than usual and eat less-healthy foods during times of stress. A poor diet contributes negatively to your reactions to stress. You should also try to eat a healthy breakfast, eat smaller portions, avoid eating large snacks after dinner, drink a lot of water, and avoid processed foods.

- **Staying in the present:** Much of the stress we feel can come from dwelling on the past or worrying about the future. To reduce this stress, you need to concentrate on the present moment. Focus all of your attention on what you are currently doing.

Not all of the techniques listed above will work for you. The key is to find ways to reduce stress and to incorporate them into your daily activities. Stress management is not a one-time-only event but a conscious daily effort. Reducing your stress can have a positive impact, not only on your job search, but also on your job performance. It can give you more energy and a more positive attitude. Respond to the following prompts to help you create a plan for managing your stress:

"Yesterday is gone. Tomorrow has not yet come. We have only today. Let us begin." —Mother Teresa

- Stress management techniques I have used in the past: _____

  _____

  _____

  _____

- New stress management techniques I would like to try: _____

  _____

  _____

  _____

- When and how I will practice these new stress management techniques:

_____

_____

_____

Managing Your Time

Managing your time is critical in your search for a job. Using good time management techniques will greatly reduce the stress you feel as you search for employment. When you feel rushed, with more to do than you have time available, it is easy to feel overwhelmed. For this activity, identify several blocks of time during the week to set aside for searching for a job. You will find that when you maintain a work schedule you will get more accomplished.

■■□ Scheduling Time and Setting Goals

Day of Week and Time of Day	Job-Search Barriers To Work On	What I Will Accomplish
_____	_____	_____
_____	_____	_____
_____	_____	_____
_____	_____	_____
_____	_____	_____
_____	_____	_____
_____	_____	_____

Dealing with Depression

Depression is a complex combination of feelings and destructive thinking. People suffering from depression find it difficult to look for a job; it can take a tremendous amount of energy to do things that were once easy. They experience a wide variety of negative emotions, including pessimism, powerlessness, and self-doubt. They focus only on the negatives in life and blame themselves and others for their situation.

The good news is that every day, doctors and researchers are discovering new ways to help people overcome depression.

Accentuate the Positive

Because depression can cause you to feel like giving up, it is important to turn your depressive thoughts into positive goals. Complete the following chart to turn your negativity into positive goal statements. An example is provided.

Negative Thoughts	Positive Goals
I cannot find a job.	Beginning tomorrow, I will work 8 hours each day contacting potential employers

In addition to working to reduce depressive thoughts, certain behaviors can also help reduce symptoms of depression. Try these techniques for alleviating your depression:

- **Continue fun activities:** When people feel sad, they often shy away from people and activities. They want to wait until the sadness passes to get back to normal daily activities. This often leads to a continued, downward spiral. It is often better to do whatever activities you enjoy. Encourage and motivate yourself to be around people and continue engaging in positive activities.

- **Take breaks:** Try to stop looking at the larger picture; it can exhaust you before you even begin a task. When you begin to feel overwhelmed, walk away for a while and relax, then come back to the task.

- **Light:** Light can be very beneficial in reversing a depressed mood. Try to spend at least a half an hour per day outside in the sunlight. You can simply walk or relax in a lounge chair. Remember that too much sunlight can be bad for your skin, so be careful. You may also want to ensure that the rooms in your home are well lit. A light-therapy box, made to treat seasonal affective disorder, mimics outdoor light and can be an effective tool when daylight is inaccessible.

Keep in mind that depression is a medical condition. While changing your attitude and behaviors can help, people experiencing depression should also seek medical assistance. A doctor can provide an accurate diagnosis and, if necessary, prescribe medications or therapy to help you cope with your depression and move on with your life and your career.

Managing Anger

You will get angry from time to time. All people do. It is a normal and often healthy human emotion. However, anger can also turn into rage, verbal abuse, or physical aggression. Anger can also interfere with your job search. It may be picked up on by employers on the phone or in interviews. It can interfere with your work, causing you to blame others or make mistakes. It is important to learn how to manage your anger so that you can be more effective, both in finding a job and on the job.

If you struggle to control feelings of anger and physical aggression, you will want to change before you hurt yourself or other people. Anger management involves learning more about the things that trigger your anger, the way you choose to express anger, and what the consequences of your anger are. If you have difficulty controlling your anger, you should first look into anger-management programs offered in your community, or consult a doctor.

However, there are a few techniques that you can use when you get angry. Many of these involve finding constructive ways to deal with stressful situations and learning to curb your initial (angry) reaction. The next time you get angry, try one of the following:

- **Take several deep breaths.** Focus on your breathing, inhaling and exhaling slowly.

- **Calm down by counting to 30.** Counting helps you to take a step back from the situation that is making you angry and buys you enough time to develop a more effective way to respond to the anger.

- **Do something physically active.** Physical activity provides an outlet for your anger.

- **Use creative visualization techniques.** By imagining yourself in a relaxing situation or a relaxing place (sitting on a dock on a calm lake), you can reduce angry feelings.

- **Identify the irrational beliefs that may be causing your anger.** This means that when you find yourself feeling angry, your thinking gets exaggerated and irrational. Try replacing these irrational thoughts with rational ones.

Take a moment to brainstorm some other strategies for managing your anger and write them in the space below.

_____

_____

_____

◼◼◻ Managing Situations When I Get Angry

Think about three things or situations that make you angry. List some strategies you will use to control your anger the next time you are in this situation.

Situations That Anger Me

1. _____

   _____

2. _____

   _____

3. _____

   _____

How I Will Control My Anger

1. _____

   _____

2. _____

   _____

3. _____

   _____

◼◼◻ Let's Talk

The way you communicate with other people is important in resolving conflicts and reducing tension with friends and family members. Use "I" statements to own your feelings and avoid blaming and criticizing others. For example, which statement will cause more conflict: "It upsets me when you do not support me when I go for job interviews" or, "It's your fault that I can't get a job"?

Also, learning to resolve conflicts is a valuable skill on the job. Being an effective communicator is one of the keys to establishing long-term career success.

Physical Barriers

Physical barriers result from physical limitations or problems. They often require a great deal of work to overcome. Some of them might be permanent, such as physical disabilities, requiring you to find ways to work around them. Physical barriers can cause you to have low self-esteem and reduce your motivation to search for employment. Physical barriers may also subject you to prejudices, stereotypes, and other social barriers.

Physical barriers can change the way you think about employment success and your performance on the job. The following sections deal with two of the most common physical barriers: physical disabilities and addictions.

Dealing with a Physical Disability

A disability is any condition that causes one to be significantly impaired as compared to the usual standard for an individual or group. A disability affects a person's ability to do daily activities such as speaking, learning, walking, working, and performing manual tasks.

■■□ Know Your Rights

If you have a disability, it's important to know your rights related to employment. The Americans with Disabilities Act (ADA) prohibits employers from discriminating against applicants on the basis of a disability unless that disability would prevent them from performing the tasks required by the job. However, the truth is that employers often will have hidden—if subconscious—biases against individuals with disabilities. The following information describes how the ADA requires employers to treat people with disabilities:

- Employers may not discriminate against an individual with a disability in hiring or promotion if the person is otherwise qualified for the job.

- Employers can ask about your ability to perform the job, but cannot ask if you have a disability or subject you to tests that will screen out people with disabilities.

- Employers will need to provide "reasonable accommodations" to you if you are disabled. Accommodations may include modification of equipment.

- Employers do not need to provide accommodations that impose an "undue hardship" on business operations.

The ADA prohibits discrimination in all types of employment situations, including job applications, hiring, firing, promotions, advancement, pay, training, and other conditions of employment.

Even though the Americans with Disabilities Act prohibits discrimination against people with disabilities, the employment rate for those with disabilities has remained relatively low. Because employers still have fears about hiring people with disabilities, you must be prepared to confront those fears. Following are several tips that may help you to find a job more easily:

- **Be realistic about your job options.** Research a variety of occupations and find the one that best fits your personality, interests, and skills, and makes allowances for your disability.

- **Take advantage of the of support services.** Agencies specializing in serving people with disabilities, such as your state Department of Vocational Rehabilitation and One-Stop Career Centers, offer valuable services.

- **Practice interviewing with a friend or family member.** These types of mock interviews will allow you to practice answering questions related to your disability.

- **Be sure that you do not put anything about your disability on your resume.** You want employers to hire you based on your ability, not your disability.

- **Focus on what you do well and not on your disability.** Do everything you can to convince employers that your disability will not interfere with your job performance.

The following exercise can help you determine those things you do well and those things you do not do well as they apply to various jobs. This can help you be realistic about your career options. More importantly, it can give you a better sense of what to focus on in the job search.

■□□ Knowing My Strengths

Think about ways that your disability may or may not limit your ability to do certain kinds of work. For each type of job, think of things you can and cannot do well and write them in the spaces provided.

Aspects of a Job	Things I Do Well	Things I Do Not Do Well
Working with data and numbers	_____	_____
	_____	_____
Working with ideas and being creative	_____	_____
	_____	_____
Working with people	_____	_____
	_____	_____
Working with tools and machines	_____	_____
	_____	_____
Performing physical or manual labor	_____	_____
	_____	_____

Thankfully there are numerous organizations and resources available to help individuals with disabilities find jobs and achieve career success. State vocational-rehabilitation agencies provide a wide range of services for people with disabilities, including counseling, medical and psychological evaluations, retraining, vocational training, transportation assistance, prostheses, and job placement services. You can find more information about your own state rehabilitation agency at http://askjan.org/cgi-win/typequery.exe?902. In addition, the following agencies and resources might also be helpful:

- ABILITYJobs (http://abilityjobs.com)
- Disability.gov (http://disability.gov)
- Enable America (http://enableamerica.org)

◼◼◻ Don't Let Anything Stand in Your Way

- Beethoven was deaf when he composed his most famous symphony.

- Thomas Edison could not read until he was about 12 years old.

- Albert Einstein had a learning disability and had trouble doing math in school.

- Franklin Roosevelt was paralyzed by polio when he was 39.

- John Milton was blind when he wrote his most famous book, *Paradise Lost.*

Whatever your disability is, you don't have to let it interfere with your success.

Dealing with Addictions

Substance abuse refers to an over-indulgence in and a dependence on one or more of a range of addictive substances, including tobacco, alcohol, illegal drugs, and prescription drugs. An addiction is a disease that negatively affects your emotions, thinking, and behavior. Addictions can lead to problems in your relationships, at home, at school, and in the workplace.

More specifically, substance abuse can affect your search for employment in a wide variety of ways, including:

- **Physically:** People who are addicted to substances fail to take adequate care of themselves. They may not get enough sleep or eat a proper diet. Thus, they are not prepared to do the work that is required in a typical job search or on the job itself.

- **Behaviorally:** People who are addicted to substances have difficulty developing and maintaining relationships. They have trouble making decisions and completing tasks. They may lack self-control as well. This makes it difficult to network and interview for jobs.

- **Emotionally:** People who are addicted to substances generally experience feelings of anxiety, fear, guilt, depression, and shame. They tend to have unexplained mood swings. They also tend to have low self-esteem.

If you have a substance-abuse problem, you might not even realize how much it is affecting your life and career. The worksheet that follows can give you a sense of the impact that your addition is having on your job search and your career success.

▮▮▯ The Effects of Abuse

A substance-abuse problem can hamper a person's job search and have a dramatic impact on his or her job performance. Take a moment to think about how your own addiction affects your employment success.

In the first column, write down any negative consequences arising from your substance abuse as it relates to each aspect of your work or job search. In the second column, list any positive outcomes that would come from overcoming your substance abuse.

Effects on My Job Search	Negative Consequences	Positive Outcomes
Finding job leads	_____	_____
Having enough energy	_____	_____
Interviewing	_____	_____
Networking	_____	_____
Keeping a positive attitude	_____	_____
Effects on My On-the-Job Success	_____	_____
Making it to work	_____	_____
Interacting with others	_____	_____
Performing my responsibilities	_____	_____
Meeting deadlines	_____	_____

If you are having a substance-abuse problem, you need to develop a recovery plan. Recovery plans usually include seeing a professional counselor to talk about your problem, using multiple types of stress-management techniques, managing your diet and health, and attending self-help programs regularly. Use the recovery resources listed below in developing your recovery plan:

- Alcoholics Anonymous (http://aa.org)

- Drug-abuse resources (http://drug-help.com)

- Help with addiction (http://helpguide.org/topics/addiction.htm)

- Narcotics Anonymous (http://na.org)

- Substance Abuse and Mental Health Services Administration (http://beta.samhsa.gov)

- US National Institute on Alcohol Abuse and Alcoholism (http://niaaa.nih.gov)

- US National Institute on Drug Abuse (http://drugabuse.gov)

List the steps you will take to help you overcome your addiction and prevent it from interfering with your job search and career success.

_____

_____

_____

_____

_____

_____

■■□ Pre-employment Drug Testing: One Test You Don't Want to Fail

It is perfectly within an employer's rights to ask you to undergo drug testing. Prospective employers want employees who will show up on time and not miss a lot of work. If you test positive for illegal substances prior to employment, you will severely hurt your chances of being employed. If you are still currently using illegal substances, now is the time to stop. Your job depends on it!

Summary

Emotional and physical barriers can interfere with all aspects of your career. Employers are concerned that people with these types of barriers will not be dependable or that the quality of their work will suffer. In addition, people with emotional and physical barriers have difficulty mustering the energy necessary to conduct successful job searches. The exercises and information in this chapter can help you begin to overcome your emotional and physical barriers. However, you should also be sure to consult professional advice if such barriers persist.

◼◼◻ Barrier Breakers

Pete is a 32-year-old pipefitter who was fired from his job after seven years of service. Pete had always had trouble managing his emotions, and his quick temper was one of the reasons he was let go. This only made him angrier. After spending three weeks unemployed, his emotions intensified until ultimately he became depressed and no longer wanted to look for a new job at all. He spent most of his time in front of the television until his wife made him get help.

After talking with a mental-health counselor, Pete realized that the first step in finding a new job was changing his attitude. That meant getting his emotions in check. He started taking more responsibility for his emotions and his actions. He attended classes on anger management offered by a community center. He started jogging 30 minutes a day, which led to more energy and less stress.

Most importantly, he learned that while there were many aspects of his life and career that were outside of his control, he could always control his reaction to them. With better control of his emotions and higher self-esteem, Pete found a job with a local contractor who also promised to help pay for him to go back to school to complete his Contractor Certification. As Pete would tell you, part of being successful is having the right perspective.

PART 3

Career Decision-Making and Planning Barriers

It can be hard to think about career planning if you are struggling to simply find a job, any job. Yet many people struggle to find work because they don't know what they are looking for. They struggle to keep jobs because they haven't thought through their career decisions.

Though they may seem less important than other barriers, career decision-making and planning barriers can have profound impacts on your current job search, as well as on your long-term success. To be successful—either finding a job or keeping one—you need to have a plan. That means thinking about your skills and interests and the kinds of work you want to do. It means exploring the career options available to you. Most importantly, it means being prepared to make good decisions.

I Don't Know What I Want

Often the first step to achieving career success is discovering work that meets your needs and matches your abilities. Knowing what you want means knowing who you are—your personality and interests. It also means knowing what you can do—the skills you have to offer an employer and that you enjoy using.

Take a moment to answer the following questions. Be honest and realistic, but don't be afraid to dream a little, either.

* What is your burning desire in life? _____

_____

_____

_____

- What things do you love doing so much that you would do them for free?

  _____

  _____

  _____

- What have you always wanted to do, but were afraid to try? _____

  _____

  _____

  _____

Your answers to the questions above will help you begin thinking about the kinds of work you would enjoy doing. That can help guide you as you search for a job or make career decisions. To make an informed career plan, however, you should take the time to assess both your interests and skills.

> Achieving your dream will take commitment, energy, and enthusiasm. Don't wait for outside forces to motivate you; find the motivation within yourself.

■■□ Have a Dream

To be successful, you must have a dream—an ultimate career goal that you want to reach. For most of us, this dream comes in the form of a career that we find interesting and enjoyable and which provides us with the lifestyle we want. Such dreams give us purpose in life. They keep us motivated. The problem with dreams is that most people don't believe they can achieve them, so they don't bother. They talk themselves out of trying.

Use the space below to visualize your dream job. Where are you? What are you doing? Whom, if anyone, are you working with? What have you accomplished? Be as specific as possible.

_____

_____

_____

_____

_____

_____

Identifying Your Interests

The key to finding long-lasting career satisfaction lies in discovering what you love to do and then finding a way to get paid for it. Unfortunately many people, maybe even you, do not know what they love to do—and most people don't know how to turn what they love into a job.

The next step, then, is to identify your interests and the types of occupations that you might enjoy. The following activity will help.

■■□ My Career Interests

The checklist below and the information that follows can help you to see how your interests relate to the world of work. It describes categories of careers grouped by interests. These categories are often called "career clusters."

Read each of the 16 descriptions carefully and then rank each cluster from 1 (most interesting to me) to 16 (least interesting to me).

Career Cluster	Description	My Ranking
Agriculture and Natural Resources	I am interested in working with plants and animals for commercial and scientific purposes. I enjoy raising, training, or grooming animals. I also enjoy growing and learning about plants, vegetables, flowers, or other natural resources.	
Architecture and Construction	I am interested in designing, assembling, and maintaining buildings and other structures. I would enjoy using hand tools, reading blueprints, operating equipment, building things, or doing manual labor.	
Arts, Audio, Video, Technology, and Communications	I am interested in expressing my feelings and ideas creatively or in communicating news and information. I enjoy performing, exhibiting, or producing entertainment content. I also am creative in writing, drawing, or designing multimedia products.	
Business and Administration	I am interested in making an organization run smoothly by directing, supervising, and coordinating the work of others. I enjoy accounting, planning, and keeping accurate records. I would enjoy providing administrative support, human resources, or business communications.	
Education and Training	I am interested in helping people to learn new things. I enjoy teaching, training, and tutoring others. I would enjoy administering or providing education and training services, or working in childcare, counseling, a library, or medical training.	

(continues)

Career Cluster	Description	My Ranking
Finance and Insurance	I am interested in helping businesses and people make sure they have financially secure futures. I would enjoy using math and financial planning for banks, insurance services, or businesses. I am also interested in financial records and trends.	
Government and Public Administration	I am interested in helping a government agency better serve the public. I enjoy managing things and making decisions. I would enjoy working in a community-service agency or regulatory service. I don't mind doing paperwork.	
Health Science	I am interested in helping people be healthy. I enjoy biology and chemistry and would enjoy providing treatment or information services in a hospital or clinic. I am also interested in doing medical research.	
Hospitality, Tourism, and Recreation	I am interested in catering to the needs and wishes of other people so that they can enjoy comfortable accommodations and have fun. I enjoy planning and staying active. I also enjoy cooking and baking for others or entertaining in my home.	
Human Services	I am interested in improving people's social, mental, emotional, and spiritual well-being. I would enjoy counseling, helping people and communities solve problems, or providing religious services.	
Information Technology	I am interested in designing, developing, and managing computers and other technology. I would like to develop and manage websites, networks, or computer programs.	
Law and Public Safety	I am interested in upholding people's rights and protecting people and property. I would like to enforce laws and regulations or help people in emergency situations.	
Manufacturing	I am interested in processing raw materials into final products, or maintaining and repairing products using machines. I would enjoy using hand tools, maintaining machinery, or working on an assembly line.	
Retail and Wholesale Sales and Service	I am interested in persuading others to do things or buy things. I enjoy promoting products, providing personal or beauty services, or raising money for causes.	
Scientific Research, Engineering, and Mathematics	I am interested in analyzing information about the natural world, life science, and human behavior. I enjoy using math and logic to solve problems and would enjoy applying scientific principles toward engineering and technology.	
Transportation, Distribution, and Logistics	I am interested in managing operations that move people or materials. I would enjoy transporting goods by road, pipeline, air, rail, or water, or provide technical support services such as planning or maintenance.	

For the three categories that you ranked the highest in the previous activity, review the jobs listed below and insert a check mark in the check box for any job that interests you. Keep in mind this is only a sample of the possible jobs in each category.

■■□ Occupations of Interest

Agriculture and Natural Resources

- ☐ Animal caretaker
- ☐ Environmental engineer
- ☐ Farmer
- ☐ Fisher
- ☐ Food scientist
- ☐ Forester
- ☐ Game warden
- ☐ Groundskeeper
- ☐ Landscape gardener
- ☐ Lawn-service manager
- ☐ Naturalist
- ☐ Park ranger
- ☐ Pest-control worker
- ☐ Soil scientist
- ☐ Veterinarian
- ☐ Wildlife biologist
- ☐ Zoologist

Architecture and Construction

- ☐ Architect
- ☐ Brickmason
- ☐ Building inspector
- ☐ Carpenter
- ☐ Draftsperson
- ☐ Floor layer
- ☐ Heating and air conditioning mechanic
- ☐ Home-appliance installer
- ☐ Painter
- ☐ Pipelayer
- ☐ Plasterer
- ☐ Plumber
- ☐ Roofer
- ☐ Sheet-metal worker
- ☐ Surveyor

Arts, Audio, Video, Technology, and Communications

- ☐ Actor
- ☐ Animator
- ☐ Camera operator
- ☐ Choreographer
- ☐ Commercial artist
- ☐ Copywriter
- ☐ Editor
- ☐ Fashion designer
- ☐ Film and video editor
- ☐ Graphic designer
- ☐ Interior designer
- ☐ Model
- ☐ Photographer
- ☐ Public relations manager
- ☐ Reporter
- ☐ Technical writer

Business and Administration

- ☐ Accountant
- ☐ Auditor
- ☐ Brokerage clerk
- ☐ Budget analyst
- ☐ Executive secretary
- ☐ File clerk
- ☐ General and operations manager
- ☐ Human-resources assistant
- ☐ Legal secretary
- ☐ Management analyst
- ☐ Medical secretary
- ☐ Meeting and convention planner
- ☐ Office clerk
- ☐ Personnel recruiter
- ☐ Postal clerk

Education and Training

- ☐ Adult-literacy teacher
- ☐ Archivist
- ☐ Curator
- ☐ Educational counselor
- ☐ Elementary school teacher
- ☐ Fitness trainer
- ☐ Instructional coordinator
- ☐ Librarian
- ☐ Library assistant
- ☐ Middle school teacher
- ☐ Preschool teacher
- ☐ Secondary school teacher
- ☐ Self-enrichment-education teacher
- ☐ Special education teacher
- ☐ Vocational education teacher

(continues)

Career Decision-Making and Planning Barriers

Finance and Insurance

- ☐ Appraiser
- ☐ Assessor
- ☐ Bank teller
- ☐ Controller
- ☐ Credit analyst
- ☐ Credit checker
- ☐ Financial advisor
- ☐ Financial analyst
- ☐ Insurance adjustor
- ☐ Insurance agent
- ☐ Insurance underwriter
- ☐ Loan clerk
- ☐ Loan officer
- ☐ Market-research analyst
- ☐ Treasurer

Government and Public Administration

- ☐ Agriculture inspector
- ☐ City-planning aide
- ☐ Court clerk
- ☐ Court reporter
- ☐ Customs agent
- ☐ Equal-opportunity representative
- ☐ Financial examiner
- ☐ Fire inspector
- ☐ Fish and game warden
- ☐ Immigration inspector
- ☐ Insurance-fraud examiner
- ☐ Licensing examiner
- ☐ Occupational safety inspector
- ☐ Revenue agent
- ☐ Urban planner

Health Science

- ☐ Athletic trainer
- ☐ Audiologist
- ☐ Chiropractor
- ☐ Dental assistant
- ☐ Massage therapist
- ☐ Medical services manager
- ☐ Occupational therapist
- ☐ Orderly
- ☐ Pharmacist
- ☐ Physical therapist
- ☐ Registered nurse
- ☐ Respiratory therapist
- ☐ Technician, laboratory
- ☐ Technician, radiology

Hospitality, Tourism, and Recreation

- ☐ Baker
- ☐ Bartender
- ☐ Chef/cook
- ☐ Counter attendant
- ☐ Food server
- ☐ Food-service manager
- ☐ Gaming manager
- ☐ Hair stylist
- ☐ Hotel/motel clerk
- ☐ Housekeeper
- ☐ Lodging manager
- ☐ Meat cutter
- ☐ Recreation worker
- ☐ Travel guide
- ☐ Umpire/referee

Human Services

- ☐ Caseworker
- ☐ Child care worker
- ☐ Clergy
- ☐ Correctional treatment specialist
- ☐ Counselor
- ☐ Funeral attendant
- ☐ Interviewer
- ☐ Nanny
- ☐ Probation officer
- ☐ Psychologist
- ☐ Recreation worker
- ☐ Rehabilitation counselor
- ☐ Social worker
- ☐ Sociologist
- ☐ Teacher's aide

Information Technology

- ☐ Amusement-machine servicer
- ☐ Computer-hardware engineer
- ☐ Computer operator
- ☐ Computer programmer
- ☐ Computer-security specialist
- ☐ Computer-support specialist
- ☐ Computer-systems analyst
- ☐ Data-processing-equipment repairer
- ☐ Database administrator
- ☐ Information systems manager
- ☐ Network systems administrator
- ☐ Office-machine servicer
- ☐ Software engineer
- ☐ Vending machine servicer

(continues)

Law and Public Safety

- ☐ Arbitrator
- ☐ Attorney
- ☐ Bailiff
- ☐ Correctional officer
- ☐ Criminal investigator
- ☐ Emergency medical technician
- ☐ Fire fighter
- ☐ Fire investigator
- ☐ Legal assistant
- ☐ Lifeguard
- ☐ Police officer
- ☐ Private detective
- ☐ Sheriff
- ☐ Title examiner

Manufacturing

- ☐ Aircraft-engine specialist
- ☐ Bookbinder
- ☐ Cabinetmaker
- ☐ Gas appliance repairer
- ☐ Industrial production manager
- ☐ Jeweler
- ☐ Machine operator
- ☐ Metal fabricator
- ☐ Molding worker
- ☐ Precision-printing technician
- ☐ Production laborer
- ☐ Tool and die maker
- ☐ Watch repairer
- ☐ Welder

Retail and Wholesale Sales and Service

- ☐ Adjustment clerk
- ☐ Advertising agent
- ☐ Advertising manager
- ☐ Buyer
- ☐ Cashier
- ☐ Funeral director
- ☐ Information clerk
- ☐ Marketing manager
- ☐ Purchasing manager
- ☐ Real-estate agent
- ☐ Rental clerk
- ☐ Retail salesperson
- ☐ Sales manager
- ☐ Sales representative
- ☐ Telemarketer

Scientific Research, Engineering, and Mathematics

- ☐ Actuary
- ☐ Astronomer
- ☐ Cartographer
- ☐ Chemist
- ☐ Engineer
- ☐ Geologist
- ☐ Historian
- ☐ Medical laboratory assistant
- ☐ Medical scientist
- ☐ Pharmacist
- ☐ Political scientist
- ☐ Radiologist
- ☐ Science teacher
- ☐ Statistician
- ☐ Surveyor

Transportation, Distribution, and Logistics

- ☐ Airplane pilot
- ☐ Ambulance driver
- ☐ Bus driver
- ☐ Chauffeur
- ☐ Courier
- ☐ Freight agent
- ☐ Freight inspector
- ☐ Locomotive engineer
- ☐ Mail carrier
- ☐ Public-transportation inspector
- ☐ Railroad conductor
- ☐ Subway operator
- ☐ Taxi driver
- ☐ Transportation manager
- ☐ Truck driver

You can start to explore your career options by researching the jobs you've just selected. But first you should take a moment to think about your skills as well.

◼◼◻ Make Your Hobbies Work for You

Your leisure activities—those things you do in your free time—are often the perfect place to start exploring career options. For example, suppose you enjoy caring for a pet in your spare time. There are many transferable skills required for this—skills that could lead to jobs. You could start boarding other people's pets for profit, learn to groom animals, go back to school to become a veterinary assistant, or open an obedience school. There are many ways to put one's leisure activity to work.

List the leisure activities you enjoy. They might include things such as gardening, playing a musical instrument, volunteering at a clinic, or working on your car. These activities will give you information about what might be your best opportunities for employment.

_____

_____

Identifying Your Skills

Knowing what skills you have to offer can help you get a job. It can also help you identify work that you would enjoy and be good at. You have hundreds of skills that could be used in a wide variety of jobs. These transferable skills may be acquired through previous jobs, hobbies, volunteer work, or education and training programs. The following exercise will help you to identify your best transferable skills.

◼◼◻ My Best Skills

We use a wide variety of skills in our work. Many of these can transfer from one job to another. Often these skills involve our ability to work with data, people, and things. Complete this exercise to help you decide what your abilities are and what kinds of jobs you might be best at.

Data

Data refers to information or knowledge that deals with both written material, such as numbers, words, and symbols, or with ideas, concepts, and interpretations. Place a check mark in the check box next to each item that represents a skill you have in working with data.

☐ Analyzing financial trends	☐ Discovering new ways to do things	☐ Inventing new products
☐ Auditing records	☐ Entering records	☐ Managing inventory
☐ Budgeting	☐ Evaluating the effectiveness of programs	☐ Proofreading documents
☐ Calculating numbers	☐ Examining finances	☐ Reporting data
☐ Classifying data	☐ Forecasting trends	☐ Reviewing data
☐ Collating information	☐ Hypothesizing theories	☐ Solving math problems
☐ Computing figures	☐ Interpreting data	☐ Synthesizing data
☐ Conceptualizing new ideas		☐ Updating information
☐ Coordinating data		☐ Word processing

(continues)

People

People refers to human beings and animals if dealt with on an individual basis. Place a check mark in the check box next to each item that represents a skill you have in working with people.

- ☐ Caring for animals
- ☐ Caring for people
- ☐ Counseling
- ☐ Demonstrating products
- ☐ Directing the work of others
- ☐ Enforcing regulations
- ☐ Entertaining people
- ☐ Interviewing people

- ☐ Making presentations
- ☐ Managing others
- ☐ Mediating conflicts
- ☐ Nursing people back to health
- ☐ Organizing events
- ☐ Promoting new ideas
- ☐ Protecting others
- ☐ Providing guidance

- ☐ Raising money
- ☐ Selling things
- ☐ Serving customers
- ☐ Speaking in public
- ☐ Teaching
- ☐ Translating languages
- ☐ Treating illnesses
- ☐ Tutoring

Things

Things refers to objects such as machines, tools, equipment, products, and materials. Place a check mark in the check box next to each item that represents a skill you have in working with things.

- ☐ Assembling things
- ☐ Binding books
- ☐ Cleaning
- ☐ Delivering materials
- ☐ Driving trucks
- ☐ Estimating distances
- ☐ Fixing electronics
- ☐ Installing equipment

- ☐ Loading boxes
- ☐ Maintaining machines
- ☐ Manipulating tools
- ☐ Monitoring machines
- ☐ Operating construction equipment
- ☐ Piloting boats
- ☐ Reading blueprints

- ☐ Repairing machines
- ☐ Servicing machines
- ☐ Sewing
- ☐ Shipping materials
- ☐ Sorting mail
- ☐ Stacking materials
- ☐ Troubleshooting problems
- ☐ Using garden tools

In which of the three categories above (Data, People, Things) do you have the most skills checked?

_____

List your top 10 transferable skills from the Data, People, and Things categories.

1. _____   6. _____

2. _____   7. _____

3. _____   8. _____

4. _____   9. _____

5. _____   10. _____

Knowing your transferable skills can help you in all aspects of your job search—from developing a resume to interviewing for jobs. But first you should use your knowledge of your interests and skills to research career options and make a plan.

I Don't Know What's Out There

There are thousands of different kinds of jobs available. Knowing your skills and interests is important, but it's just as important to understand how they match up with job opportunities. That requires doing research on careers that interest you.

⬛⬛⬜ Understanding the World of Work

The workplace of today is ever changing. New technology is creating new opportunities and new problems. Entire industries are booming as a result of this technology, including computer software development, biotechnology, and wireless telecommunications. Computers have made it easier to outsource work or to work from home. Many jobs—such as telephone operators, locomotive engineers, and coal miners—have almost ceased to exist.

As jobs in manufacturing disappear, more and more jobs open up in the service industries. Most of the jobs that are growing require some form of postsecondary education, suggesting the need for a more educated workforce (see Part 5). Globalization also changes the kinds of jobs available, as more and more jobs are outsourced to other countries.

In the future, many workers will change jobs more frequently. More workers will be required to move to get jobs. Workers will also be expected to retrain or go back to school to learn new skills.

While these and other trends may not seem important, they do have an impact on your job search. They help dictate the kinds of jobs that are available to you and how secure those jobs will be. They also can give you clues as to your career direction. Paying attention to what's hot and what's not in the world of work can help put you on the path to success.

Once you have a better idea of the kinds of jobs you are interested in, you need to research them to see if they are worth pursuing. Does the job you're interested in pay well? Are there openings available? Do you have the education required? What are the working conditions like?

One of the best ways to learn about different jobs is to read about them. The following sources can provide you with most everything you need to know to begin exploring careers of interest:

- *Occupational Outlook Handbook (OOH):* Providing written descriptions of 270 jobs, the *OOH* covers about 90% of all workers. It provides information on earnings, training required, projected growth, work environment, related jobs, and more. The *OOH* is updated every few years by the US Department of Labor. It is published by JIST and is also available online at http://www.bls.gov/OOH.

- ***O*NET Dictionary of Occupational Titles:*** Also developed and updated by the Department of Labor, this reference is based on the O*NET (Occupational Information Network) database and contains descriptions of 900 jobs. It is published by JIST and is also available online at http://onetonline.org.

- ***New Guide for Occupational Exploration (GOE):*** This reference organizes jobs into the 16 major interest groups used in this workbook. It includes details on the type of work experience, skills, and abilities needed; training and education required; and sources of additional information. The *GOE* is published by and available from JIST.

There are many other ways to explore your career options. Following are just a few of the most common:

- Speak with people who work at the kinds of jobs you are interested in. If possible, try to set up informational interviews. An *informational interview* is an educational conversation between a job seeker and a person with work experience. Informational interviews are an excellent way for job seekers to learn about career paths, get advice, network, and potentially learn about job opportunities.

- Shadow someone at a job you are interested in. That means observing them at work (without getting in the way).

- Visit websites that help you to explore your career options. Good places to start include http://careeronestop.org/StudentsandCareerAdvisors and http://acinet.org.

- Talk to career counselors or job-placement specialists for information on jobs that are available in your area.

Regardless of which methods you choose, it's important to find out as much as you can about jobs that interest you. You will use this information to make informed career decisions.

Use the worksheet that follows to help you gather information about occupations that interest you. Feel free to make multiple copies. You may gather this information from job descriptions in books, through websites, or by talking to people who work in the occupations.

> Life is a journey made of choices. How your life is in the future depends on the quality of the choices you make now.

◼◼◻ Occupational Information Sheet

Occupation/job title: _____

Duties and responsibilities: _____

_____

_____

Nature of the work: _____

_____

_____

Where is the work done? _____

How would the work allow you to express your interests? _____

_____

_____

What are the typical working hours? _____

What is the average salary? _____

What is the potential for advancement? _____

What is the long-term outlook for the occupation? _____

What kind of education or training is required? _____

_____

Things you think you would like most about the job: _____

_____

_____

Things you think you would like least about the job: _____

_____

_____

I Don't Know How to Get There

Exploring your career options can be fun and exciting. Choosing from those options is often more difficult. Career decisions require careful thought and both short- and long-term planning. That requires setting goals and identifying the steps necessary to achieve them.

Career Decision Making

During a typical day you make hundreds of choices. Some choices are small (What do I wear today?), while others are quite large (Should I quit my job and look for something better?). We can't step back and plan for every choice that we make in life, but important decisions about our career deserve careful analysis.

Effective decisions bring us closer to our goals and dreams. They help us take control of our destiny and empower us to make changes. However, many people face barriers to effective decision-making. These barriers include the fear of failure, fear of the unknown, and fear of what others will say. These fears often cause people to make poor choices or no choice at all.

What are some of your current fears with regards to your career? _____

_____

_____

_____

The best way to face these fears is to have a process in place to ensure your decisions are right for you. Such a decision-making process consists of several steps:

Step 1: Identify that there is a decision to be made and understand what is at stake.

Step 2: Gather relevant information needed to make an effective and timely decision.

Step 3: Identify alternatives or paths of action to take based on the information that you have gathered. List all possibilities.

Step 4: Weigh each alternative based on the information you have already gathered.

Step 5: Choose the alternative that provides you the best possible outcome, with a realistic amount of effort and resources.

Step 6: Take action.

Step 7: Evaluate whether or not your decision was a good one. If not, consider going back to Step 1.

Use the following worksheet to guide you through the decision-making process. Think about your current employment situation and then evaluate all of your options. Use the questions to help you figure out what to do next.

■■□ My Career Decision

Where do I currently stand in my job/career? _____

_____

_____

Where would I like to be? _____

_____

_____

What can I change to get there? _____

_____

_____

What information do I need to make an effective decision? _____

_____

_____

What are my possible choices? _____

_____

_____

Of those possibilities, which *two* seem the most likely to lead to success? _____

_____

_____

Of those two choices, which am I the most committed to right now? _____

_____

How can I implement this decision? _____

_____

_____

It is important to see things as they really are. You cannot change the past, but you can influence your future. No matter what you may finally choose to change, simply understanding that you do have a choice in how your life plays out is empowering.

<aside>Always consider your long-term plan for career success, even when making short-term decisions.</aside>

Setting Goals

The best decisions in the world are worthless without the motivation to act on them. By making a strong commitment to your choices, you create your own motivation. But you must also set purposeful goals to help you maintain your motivation.

There are two types of goals: short-term and long-term. *Short-term goals* describe what you would like to accomplish within the next few months. *Long-term goals* describe what you would like to accomplish within the next year or more. Short-term goals are often stepping stones toward the achievement of your long-term goals.

Defining your goals is a critical part of reaching them. To make your goals effective, be sure that

- they are yours, not someone else's;

- they are stated in as specific, measurable terms as possible;

- they have observable outcomes so that you know when you've achieved them;

- they are realistic and attainable; otherwise, you set yourself up for failure; and

- they are positive and stated positively—focus on what you *want* to do, rather than what you do *not* want to do.

Also be sure your goals have specific deadlines. By setting dates, you can maintain your motivation and energy. But remember to keep your dates realistic.

■■□ Think Long, Act Short

Short-term goals can keep you energized and motivated to reach your long-term ones. Long-term goals are those that extend far—even decades—into the future. These goals may change over time and are the most difficult to achieve. For this reason, you should concentrate your efforts on your short-term goals. Short-term goals tend to be more flexible, be more easily achieved, keep you motivated, provide direction, and provide guidelines for future action.

Take a moment to set some short-term and long-term goals for your career. An effective short-term goal might be, "I will get three interviews by the end of the month." Notice that this goal is specific and measurable. It is realistic and also has a deadline.

An effective long-term goal might be, "I will start my own small business within five years." As stepping stones to this long-term goal, you would then set a series of short-term goals. Examples of short-term goals to keep you on track to starting your own business might include the following:

- "Identify the type of small business I would like to start by the end of next week."

- "Read two library books about starting a small business by the end of the month."

- "Talk with small business owners in the community over the next three months."

- "Do a market survey to see about the viability of this type of business by the end of the year."

■■□ My Goals

In the spaces below, list your own long-term goals. Avoid vague goals such as, "I want to make a lot of money." Instead, these goals should be as specific and as precise as possible. An example is provided.

Within 10 years I will be making at least $35,000, with full benefits.

1. _____

_____

2. _____

_____

3. _____

_____

List short-term goals that will act as stepping stones to attaining each of your long-term goals.

Short-term goals for achieving long-term goal #1: _____

_____

_____

_____

(continues)

Short-term goals for achieving long-term goal #2: _____

_____

_____

Short-term goals for achieving long-term goal #3: _____

_____

_____

_____

Once they are set, you need to take responsibility for achieving your goals. You, and only you, must be responsible for their completion.

Taking Action

People who are unemployed or who are struggling to find success on the job need to do more than dream. They cannot wait for something to happen to them or wait until the very last moment to take action. They must put themselves in a position to make those dreams come true. You will need to be persistent to achieve your goals. It takes time, energy, and self-discipline to follow through on your decisions.

> "I can't change the direction of the wind, but I can adjust my sails to always reach my destination." —Jimmy Dean

One of the best ways to motivate yourself to action is to visualize what you will do by writing out action statements. An action statement is what you will *do* in order to achieve your short-term goal. Following are some examples of action statements:

- "I will register to take a class at the community college next semester."

- "I will go to the library next week and find out all I can about the occupation of computer-aided drafting."

- "I will set up an informational interview with a heating and air-conditioning technician before the end of the month."

When you are writing action statements, you should always begin with "I will" and always list a time by which you will complete the action. This will keep you motivated and prevent you from procrastinating.

Career Decision-Making and Planning Barriers

Ready, Set, Action!

Take one of the short-term goals you listed earlier and write it in the space provided. For your selected short-term goal, write three action statements that you could do to move closer to this goal. Do the same for two other short-term goals you'd like to reach.

My Short-Term Goal #1: _____

Action Statements

1. _____

2. _____

3. _____

My Short-Term Goal #2: _____

Action Statements

1. _____

2. _____

3. _____

My Short-Term Goal #3: _____

Action Statements

1. _____

2. _____

3. _____

Summary

Few people will say that making career decisions is easy, but all will say that it is worth it. Planning a successful career means eliminating your fears—and that means knowing as much about yourself and your options as possible. The more you learn about yourself and begin to tie your skills to occupations that interest you, the more motivated you will be. With motivation comes even more career success.

■■□ Barrier Breakers

Hector was not happy in his work. He got certified in computer-aided drafting because people told him he would have a secure future in this field and make good money. They didn't tell him how sick he'd get of sitting behind a desk. They didn't tell him he would  hate getting up in the morning. They didn't tell him to find work he would enjoy or that would let him feel motivated and fulfilled.

Hector wanted a more active job, something physical, but that fit with his values and his desire to help people. He said he always dreamed about being a cop but never thought he could achieve that dream.

Finally he got fed up staring at his computer screen all day and looked into what would be required to become a police officer. He enrolled in a criminal justice program at his local community college, taking classes online and in the evenings. With his degree in hand, he is now thinking about going to police academy.

Hector will be the first to tell you that working just any job won't do. To have a successful career, you need to find work that you are passionate about. It might take some work to get there—but it will be worth it.

PART 4

Job-Search Knowledge Barriers

Many of the barriers already discussed not only stand in the way of getting a job, they stand in the way of even *looking* for one. But if you can overcome *those* barriers—if you can meet your basic needs and create a support network, improve your attitude and make a solid career plan—then you are ready to go out and find a good job quickly.

Finding a job becomes easier if you break it down into simple steps. These steps include understanding the job market, finding job openings, writing a resume, filling out applications, interviewing, and following up. Finding a job requires that you not only understand these steps, but that you develop the skills required to take them.

This section contains many practical job-search strategies, samples, notes, and exercises to help you overcome any barriers you might have and minimize the time you spend finding work.

Understanding the Job Market

For many, searching for a job simply means sending out hundreds of resumes in the hope that someone will give them work. This "hit-or-miss" approach to finding a job usually results in lengthy job searches or having to accept positions that they have no interest in.

There are better ways to find a job. To better understand the job market, you need to understand the two basic types of jobs you can look for: *visible* and *hidden* jobs.

Knowing Versus Doing

You might already know how to conduct a job search. You may know all about networking and interviewing and writing an effective resume. Sometimes it's not knowing *how* to do something that stands in your way, it's having the energy, motivation, and confidence actually to *do* it. If your problem is not a lack of knowledge but a lack of drive, you should go back and review the barriers discussed in the previous sections of the workbook.

The Visible Job Market

Most people struggle to find jobs because they only look in the *visible* job market. *Visible* job leads are those openings that have been officially announced by an organization. Employers traditionally make the public aware of these openings by placing ads in newspapers and on the Internet, announcing them internally, and alerting employment offices and government agencies.

Most job seekers only try for jobs that have been announced. Thus, there is more competition for visible jobs, and that makes them harder to get. This isn't to say that you can't find a job in the visible job market, only that you shouldn't concentrate all of your time and energy looking for jobs that have been advertised. To get the most out of the visible job market, consider the following sources of visible job leads:

> The next time you open up the newspaper classifieds or search for jobs online, stop and think about all the other people who are doing the same thing. They are your competition. Wouldn't it be better to go after jobs that *they* don't know about yet?

- **Newspaper/Internet want ads:** Most companies advertise openings in the want ads. Just remember all the other people who are reading and answering the same ads that you are.

- **Employment agencies:** These are agencies that match employees with prospective employers. These agencies are paid a fee for their services. In some cases, the company pays the employment agency's fees. In others, the person getting the job agrees to pay a percentage of his or her wages in return for the agency's help. Make sure you understand the costs of using such a service.

> Most organizations you might want to work for will have a website. Many companies include job postings as part of their online recruitment strategies. Don't overlook these valuable sources when looking for a job.

- **Chambers of commerce:** Your local chamber of commerce can be a good source for identifying employers in your community. It also publishes a list of new companies in the area.

- **Libraries:** The library is a great place to start researching prospective employers. Ask your librarian for a list of good resources.

- **State employment/job-service office:** These are agencies that assist job seekers with unemployment benefits, job placement, and on-the-job training. You should register with the office in your area. To find your local office, go online to http://servicelocator.org/OWSLinks.asp.

In addition to the sources listed above, a Career Information Delivery System (CIDS) can also be very useful electronic resources to use in your search for employment. CIDSes typically provide a variety of sorting and searching services, including

- descriptions of various occupations of interest;

- information about educational programs and educational institutions;

- one or more instruments for identifying skills, interests, and values and then relating those to occupations; and

- links to other helpful resources.

A CIDS program can be national or state-based. One national CIDS program is CareerOneStop at http://careeronestop.org. State-based CIDS programs include most aspects of the national CIDS programs, but also offer information about employers, local jobs, and training opportunities.

■■□ Computers and the Job Search

The Internet has transformed the way that people look for jobs. Most notably, you can look for openings and post your resume on hundreds of job-search sites. Following are some of the more common:

- America's Job Bank (http://americasjobbank.com)

- CareerBuilder (http://careerbuilder.com)

- Glassdoor (http://glassdoor.com)

- Indeed (http://indeed.com)

- LinkedIn (http://linkedin.com)

- Monster (http://monster.com)

- SimplyHired (http://simplyhired.com)

- USAjobs (http://usajobs.gov)

With any of these job banks, you can search for jobs by location, keyword, or job type. You can then apply for positions or post your resume online for employers to see.

But don't just wait for them to contact you. Because of the volume of resumes received, it can be difficult to stand out in the crowd. Therefore, you should always pursue the more active approaches to your job search.

Keep in mind that you do not need your own computer to have a successful job search. Friends or family members may let you use their computer. If not, most libraries have computers that you can use for free. You will need regular access to email so you can respond to prospective employers.

List the strategies you have already used to access the visible job market. Also write down two or three strategies you plan to use in the future:

- Strategies I'm using now: _____

_____

_____

Job-Search Knowledge Barriers

- Strategies I will start using: _____

_____

_____

_____

The Hidden Job Market

Hidden job leads are those openings you aren't aware of because they haven't been announced yet. The key to finding hidden jobs is to make contact with the people who make hiring decisions in companies you'd like to work for. When a job *does* become available, they will already know who you are and consider you for it. The two best methods for tapping the hidden job market are making direct contact and networking.

> Nobody wants to hire someone who is gloomy, negative, or angry. Remember that you must keep a positive attitude if you are to be successful in finding—and keeping—a job.

Making Direct Contact   Nearly half of all people get their jobs through networking, direct mail, and phone campaigns. In short, they call potential employers and ask to meet with them to discuss both current and future job opportunities. To be successful with your campaign, you should take the following steps:

1. **Research and screen organizations of interest.** Find companies you'd like to work for. Research them using some of the sources mentioned previously in this section or look them up on the Internet. Make sure that each company is one that could make use of your skills and experience.

2. **Identify hiring officials in these organizations.** Try to identify the hiring official through your Internet research. If you are unable to find the hiring official this way, call or email the company and request this information from the operator or secretary. Usually this is the manager of the department you would want to work for. Avoid speaking to the human resources (HR) department if possible.

3. **Send a well-crafted cover letter and resume.** Be sure these are customized for each employer you are interested in. Address your cover letter specifically to the hiring official.

4. **Make your phone presentation.** Call the hiring official two to three days after your resume and cover letter arrive. Prepare a phone script to help guide you.

5. **Ask for an interview.** This is most important. Even if there are no jobs currently available, ask if you can come in to present your skills and discuss the possibility of future openings.

■■□ Using a Phone Script to Contact Employers

Contacting employers by phone can be difficult. It is often less threatening to mail or email a resume or post one online, but this is less likely to result in an interview. By using the telephone effectively, you can interact more directly with employers and give them a better impression of you.

Following is a sample conversation of a job seeker asking an employer for an interview:

Job Seeker: "Hello, my name is Maya Brown. I'm interested in a position as an administrative assistant in your office, and I would like to meet with you to discuss job openings. I have two years of experience as a legal secretary. I am proficient in customer care, word processing, and database management. I also have an associate's degree in business administration. Would it be possible for us to meet tomorrow to discuss possible job openings or would some other time next week be better for you?"

Employer: "Sorry, we just don't have any openings at this time."

Job Seeker: "I understand. But I would still like to speak with you about any future openings. Would it be possible to schedule an informational interview?

Employer: "All right. Let's set something up for early next week."

The following exercise can help you develop a phone script that might make the process of contacting employers by phone easier and less frightening. In this exercise, you will plan what you might say to an employer. Be concise and sincere. Practice this phone call with friends or relatives. Your exact wording will vary, but you can follow this basic script with every telephone contact you make.

Greeting and introduction: _____

_____

_____

Reason for call: _____

_____

_____

Tell about your experience/education, skills, and personality: _____

_____

_____

_____

_____

_____

(continues)

Closing (ask for an interview): _____

_____

_____

Networking   Have you ever felt that it's not *what* you know but *whom* you know that determines who gets a job? Many people find work simply by asking the people they already know for job leads. *Networking* is the process of meeting people who can provide you with information that may lead to a job.

 Use the following worksheet to get you started thinking about your network. Remember, though, that building a network is hard work. Still, networking is often the best way to find hidden jobs.

■■□ Building Your Network

A network is made up of people you currently know and people you will soon meet. You should be able to generate an initial network of 10 or more people.

 Identify your current network of contacts. Contacts are people you already know, such as friends, relatives, people with whom you have worked, past teachers, acquaintances, etc. In the following section, list anyone who could help you find a job. List their phone numbers and email addresses, if you have them. Feel free to use a separate sheet of paper to add to your list.

Name	Phone Number	Email Address
_____	_____	_____
_____	_____	_____
_____	_____	_____
_____	_____	_____
_____	_____	_____
_____	_____	_____

 Identify contacts for prospective employers. List employers you would like to work for. Also list the name(s) of people who could provide you with a potential contact in each of the companies you list. If you can't think of anyone, write down the name of the hiring authority in that organization.

(continues)

```
Employer 1: _____

_____

Employer 2: _____

_____

Employer 3: _____

_____
```

You can also build your network by going to community events and joining professional societies. Get involved in social organizations such as athletic clubs, charitable groups, and church groups. The more people you interact with, the better your chances of meeting someone who can help you find a job.

■■□ Informational Interviewing

One way to build a network of contacts is through informational interviewing. Informational interviews help you research careers you are interested in by talking to people about their jobs.

During an informational interview, you will want to find out as much as you can about the person's job, including how they prepared for and got it. Informational interviews are usually brief (no more than 30 minutes) and less formal than employment interviews. Be sure to have specific questions prepared that you want to ask, but never ask for a job—just advice.

At the end of the interview, you should ask for the names of at least three additional contacts. Always be sure to send a thank-you note to the person who interviewed you.

Social Networking *Social networking* is an electronic form of networking in which you use social media sites to search for jobs, develop your "brand" profile for prospective employers, and communicate electronically with people who have similar interests and skills as you. Some of the more popular social media sites for job seekers include LinkedIn (http://linkedin.com) and Twitter (http://twitter.com).

> The Internet provides many resources to help job seekers. For example, Glassdoor (http://glassdoor.com) provides company reviews, salary information, interview reviews, blogs, and other resources.

Some tips for using social media effectively include:

- For any social media site you use, develop a profile and keep your profile up to date. In developing your profile, use as many industry keywords as possible.

- If you want to write about your employment interests, you can begin your own blog at sites such as http://wordpress.com.

- Use social media sites to gather research about organizations and people with whom you interview.

- Join groups within social media to network with people who have interests similar to your own.

- Many social media sites, like LinkedIn, provide search engines for you to look for employment in your community.

Resumes, Cover Letters, and Job Applications

If you are like most people, you hate the idea of sitting down and writing a resume. But there's no escaping the fact that having an effective resume and cover letter are critical in your search for employment. They should present a positive, professional image.

Writing Your Resume

Your resume is an overview of the skills, experience, and education that you have to offer an employer. Most employers use resumes as screening tools to narrow down the hundreds or thousands of potential candidates to the handful they want to interview. In general, your resume has less than a minute to convince an employer to interview you.

> The job search is a process, not a single event. You will rarely find a job as quickly as you like. Be prepared for ups and downs.

If you have struggled with writing resumes and cover letters, consider the following barriers and the suggestions for overcoming them. Check off any that apply to you, and then try to think of additional ways that you can overcome those barriers.

☐ **Lack of experience.** Some people just don't feel like they have anything worthwhile to put on a resume. If that's the case, consider drawing on your experiences from a variety of other roles. Work experience can come from a number of different places, including hobbies, volunteer activities, leadership activities, or prison work assignments. You can use these types of experiences (and the transferable skills gained from working at them) to develop a functional resume and answer interview questions.

☐ **Problems with writing or with the English language.** If you struggle with writing, or if you are learning English as a secondary language, consider getting assistance from a counselor at your local employment office, begin taking some English-language learner classes, or join an English conversation group in your community. In addition, local YMCAs and libraries often offer classes to help people with writing and speaking English.

☐ **Lack of computer skills.** Nearly all resumes and cover letters are typed and formatted using computers. This requires basic knowledge of word processing programs such as Microsoft Word. If you lack these basic computer skills, consider taking a computer literacy class at a local community college or attend a seminar offered at a local library. Many adult-education programs offer these basic courses at little or no cost.

☐ **Lack of resources.** Often people simply don't know what an effective resume or cover letter *looks* like. While this workbook provides a few examples, there are hundreds of other resources that can provide examples to guide you. The following are just a few books to get you started:

- *The Quick Resume & Cover Letter Book*, Michael Farr

- *Résumé Magic*, Susan Whitcomb

- *The Everything Resume Book*, Burton Nadler

Just as all people are different from one another, all resumes should be different. Beware of copying a friend's resume or a sample resume you find in any book. Your resume must be tailor-made to fit your strengths.

The following information is found, in one form or another, in most resumes:

> Gaps in the work experience section of your resume can be filled by listing volunteer work or self-employment.

- **Identifying information:** This should include your name, present address (including ZIP code), telephone number (including area code), and email address (if you have one; if you don't, you should get one).

- **Job objective:** Include a specific statement that identifies the type of position you are applying for.

- **Education:** You should list schools you have attended or training programs you have completed (identifying the most recent first). Be sure to list degrees or certificates received, major(s) and minor(s), and the date(s) of graduation/completion.

- **Work experience:** Include a summary of your work experience, emphasizing the most recent or most important job relevant to your job objective. Work backward and include all types of work experience (full-time employment, volunteer experiences, summer employment, part-time employment, internships, etc.). List the title of your position, name of employer, dates of employment, and describe the nature of your work in detail.

- **Interests, activities, and honors:** Prospective employers *are* interested in your leisure activities (especially if they are directly related to your job objective). Identify any organizations you belong to and any offices you hold in those organizations. Also include any honors or awards you have received.

- **References:** State that letters of reference will be "available upon request" or leave this information off completely. You will need them, however, so select three individuals who are familiar with your qualifications and ask them if they would be willing to write you favorable letters of reference. These references can be former employers, supervisors, coworkers, long-time acquaintances, or instructors.

In an effective resume, both content *and* presentation matter. A sloppy or poorly designed resume often won't get looked at. A resume that is full of spelling errors will be thrown away. Take some time to carefully edit your resume. Show it to others. Take it to your local employment office and ask them to look it over. Make certain that it looks professional and reflects the best in you.

Consider the following when editing your resume:

- Check your spelling, grammar, and punctuation. After you feel it is error free, ask two or three other people double-check it. Misspellings and typographical errors suggest that you are careless and inattentive to detail.

- Leave adequate margins on each side (one-inch margins are recommended).

- Single-space the text within the resume.

- Keep your resume to one page, possibly two pages if you have a lot of work experience.

- Emphasize important aspects of your resume by using boldface type, uppercasing letters, and underlining words.

- Use bullet points to highlight skills, responsibilities, and accomplishments.

- Don't crowd too much information on your resume. Leave considerable "white space" (empty space) so that your resume is easy to read.

- Be sure to print your resume on high-quality paper, preferably white or off-white.

You can use the sample resumes that follow as general guides for developing your own. The first is a more traditional, chronological resume that emphasizes work experience. The second is a functional resume that emphasizes skills—a good format to use if you have limited work experience. The third is a combination of those two types.

Judith J. Jones

115 South Hawthorne Avenue
Chicago, IL 66204

jj@emcp.net
(312) 555-9217 (cell)

JOB OBJECTIVE

A position requiring excellent business management expertise in an office environment. Position should require a variety of skills, including office management, word processing, and spreadsheet and database application use.

EDUCATION AND TRAINING

Acme Business College, Lincoln, IL
Completed one-year program in **Professional Office Management.** Achieved GPA in top 30% of class. Courses included word processing, accounting theory and systems, advanced spreadsheet and database applications, graphics design, time management, and supervision.

John Adams High School, South Bend, IN
Graduated with emphasis on **business courses**. Earned excellent grades in all business topics and won top award for word-processing speed and accuracy.

Other: Continuing-education programs at own expense, including business communications, customer relations, computer applications, and sales techniques.

EXPERIENCE

2012–present—**Claims Processor, Blue Spear Insurance Company,** Wilmette, IL. Process 50 complex medical insurance claims per day, almost 20% above department average. Created a spreadsheet report process that decreased department labor costs by more than $30,000 a year. Received two merit raises for performance.

2011–2012—**Returned to business school to gain advanced office skills.**

2008–2011—**Finance Specialist (E4), US Army.** Systematically processed more than 200 invoices per day from commercial vendors. Trained and supervised eight employees. Devised internal system allowing 15% increase in invoices processed with a decrease in personnel. Managed department with a budget equivalent of more than $350,000 a year. Honorable discharge.

2007–2008—**Sales Associate promoted to Assistant Manager, Sandy's Boutique,** Wilmette, IL. Made direct sales and supervised four employees. Managed daily cash balances and deposits, made purchasing and inventory decisions, and handled all management functions during owner's absence. Sales increased 26% and profits doubled during tenure.

2005–2007—**Held various part-time and summer jobs through high school while maintaining GPA 3.0/4.0.** Earned enough to pay all personal expenses, including car insurance. Learned to deal with customers, meet deadlines, work hard, and handle multiple priorities.

STRENGTHS AND SKILLS

Reliable, with strong work ethic. Excellent interpersonal, written, and oral communication and math skills. Accept supervision well, effectively supervise others, and work well as a team member. General ledger, accounts payable, and accounts receivable expertise. Proficient in Microsoft Word, Excel, PowerPoint, and Outlook; WordPerfect.

Lisa M. Rhodes

813 Lava Court • Denver, CO 81613
Home: (413) 555-2173 (leave message)
Cell: (413) 555-1659
lrhodes@emcp.net

Objective

Sales-oriented position in a retail sales or distribution business.

Skills and Abilities

Communications	Good written and verbal presentation skills. Uses proper grammar and have a good speaking voice.
Interpersonal Skills	Able to get along well with coworkers and accept supervision. Received positive evaluations from previous supervisors.
Flexible	Willing to try new things and am interested in improving efficiency on assigned tasks.
Attention to Detail	Concerned with quality. Produce work that is orderly and attractive. Ensure tasks are completed correctly and on time.
Hardworking	Throughout high school, worked long hours in strenuous activities while attending school full-time. Often managed as many as 65 hours a week in school and other structured activities while maintaining above-average grades.
Customer Service	Routinely handled as many as 500 customer contacts a day (10,000 per month) in a busy retail outlet. Averaged lower than a .001% complaint rate and was given the "Employee of the Month" award in second month of employment. Received two merit increases.
Cash Sales	Handled more than $2,000 a day ($40,000 a month) in cash sales. Balanced register and prepared daily sales summary and deposits.
Reliable	Excellent attendance record; trusted to deliver daily cash deposits totaling more than $40,000 a month.

Education

Franklin High School, 2007–2011. Classes included advanced English. Member of award-winning band. Excellent attendance record. Superior communication skills. Graduated in top 30% of class.

Other

Active gymnastics competitor for four years. Learned discipline, teamwork, how to follow instructions, and hard work. Ambitious, outgoing, reliable, and have solid work ethic.

DENISE A. WOLFE

7102 Dalewood Court — Nashville, Tennessee 68321 — (615) 555-2922 — dawolfe@emcp.net

SUMMARY OF QUALIFICATIONS

- **REGISTERED DENTAL ASSISTANT** with 10 years' experience assisting with direct patient care. Special interest in pediatric patient care, with the desire and willingness to learn other areas of dentistry.

- Graduate of Dental Assistant program at Volunteer State Community College. Continuing dental education in coronal polishing. CPR certified.

- Special expertise in patient management and making patients of all ages feel as relaxed and comfortable as possible, relieving any anxiety or tension they might have. Skilled working with handicapped and other special-needs patients.

- Sound knowledge of clinical procedures and dental/medical terminology.

DENTAL HEALTH CARE EXPERIENCE

DENTAL ASSISTANT .... 2013 to 2015
David A. Lambert, D.D.S. — Montgomery, Alabama

- Performed general chairside duties (four-handed dentistry) and assisted with all types of procedures, including extraction, crowns, pulpotomy, and composites. Monitored nitrous oxide and applied topical anesthetics.
- Prepared patients (children, adolescents, young adults, handicapped, special needs) for treatment, making them as comfortable and at ease as possible. Assisted with in-hospital visits and procedures.
- Performed coronal polishing, oral examinations, and charting.
- Sterilized instruments and equipment. Prepared tray setups for procedures.
- Mixed amalgams, cements, and other dental materials. Took and poured impressions.
- Took, processed, and mounted x-rays. Used intraoral camera equipment.
- Scheduled and confirmed appointments. Ordered dental supplies and maintained inventory levels.

DENTAL ASSISTANT .... 2010 to 2013
Timothy J. Koeppel, D.M.D. — Hendersonville, Tennessee

- Took impressions, poured and trimmed models, and made night guards.
- Took and processed panorex and cephalometric x-rays.
- Instructed and encouraged patients to develop good oral-hygiene habits.

EDUCATION AND TRAINING

Coronal Polishing — Continuing Dental Education — 2011
University of Tennessee, Memphis College of Dentistry - Memphis, Tennessee
Dental Assistant Certificate of Proficiency — 2009
Volunteer State Community College - Gallatin, Tennessee
Certified in CPR through American Heart Association — 2007 to Present

Writing Your Cover Letter

You will want to include a cover letter with each resume you send to employers. Cover letters introduce your resume and highlight aspects of your background. A well-written cover letter can ensure that your resume gets looked at.

Your cover letter should be specifically adapted to each job that you apply for. However, most cover letters contain the following parts:

- **Heading:** Include your personal contact information, the address of the organization you are applying to, and the current date.

- **Formal greeting:** Addressed specifically to the person with the authority to hire you.

- **Introduction:** The introductory paragraph compels the employer to read the rest of the letter. It should tell him or her a little bit about yourself and why you are writing. It should also mention any mutual contacts.

- **"Summary of qualifications" paragraph:** Indicate why you are interested in the position and the organization and the value you can bring to it. Create interest by explaining how your unique qualities and characteristics make you a qualified candidate. Be sure to emphasize any education or work experience that will help you in the position.

- **Closing paragraph:** In the last paragraph, state your appreciation for the person's time and indicate your desire for an interview. Include your phone number. If possible, close your letter with a statement or question that will initiate follow-up plans.

- **Closing:** Generally "Sincerely," and your name, both typed and signed, works best.

The following exercise will help you draft a cover letter of your own. Feel free to use the example on page 72 as a guide, but don't just copy what you find there. Make your letter about your own unique skills and experiences.

■■□ Cover Letter Draft Form

First Paragraph: State why you are writing the letter and how you found out about the position or learned about the organization.

_____

_____

_____

_____

_____

(continues)

Second Paragraph: Indicate why you are interested in the position, the company, its products or services, and above all, what you can do for the employer. Be sure to summarize and highlight your key strengths and abilities.

_____

_____

_____

_____

_____

Final Paragraph: State your appreciation and indicate your desire for a personal interview.

_____

_____

_____

_____

Filling Out Applications

In many cases, an application is the first contact you will have with a prospective employer. Employment applications are basic forms used by organizations to "screen out" unqualified job applicants. Therefore, it must be as impressive and accurate as it can be. The following tips can help you overcome common barriers people face when completing applications:

- Think before you write. If at all possible, take the application home and complete it. This will give you more time to ensure the information you provide is accurate and complete.

- Never write "See Resume" on the application in lieu of answering all the questions.

- Read all instructions carefully before you begin. If there is something on the form you do not understand, ask for assistance or call the personnel office for clarification.

> The only individuals who don't experience rejection in the job market are those who don't even try to look for a job. Don't take rejection personally. Remember that failing to get a particular job does not make you a failure.

947 Cherry Street
Middleville, Ohio 01234

October 22, 2016

Mr. Alfred E. Newman, President
Alnew Consolidated Stores, Inc.
1 Newman Place
New City, OK 03000

Dear Mr. Newman:

I am interested in the position of national sales director, which you recently advertised in the *Retail Sales and Marketing* newsletter.

I am very familiar with your company's innovative marketing techniques, as well as your enlightened policy in promoting and selling environmentally sound merchandise nationwide. I have been active for some time now in environmental-protection projects, both as a representative of my current employer and on my own. I recently successfully introduced a new line of kitchen products that exceeds federal standards, is environmentally safe, and is selling well.

The enclosed resume outlines my experience and skills in both sales and marketing in the retail field. I would like to meet with you to discuss how my skills would benefit Alnew Consolidated Stores. I will contact you soon to request an interview for current or future positions and may be reached at (513) 555-6543.

Thank you for your time and consideration.

Sincerely,

Robin Redding

- Always print all information on the application form, except your signature. Use black or blue ink and never use pencil. There should be no visible erasures, and no words crossed out.

- Print as neatly as possible. If it is neat and accurate, employers will assume *you* are neat and accurate.

- Spell all words correctly. If possible, carry a pocket dictionary with you or check spelling via a smartphone when you apply.

- Be honest. Most applications have statements that indicate that if you provide false information to an employer, you can be fired. Remember that employers will check the information you provide for accuracy.

Conducting a Successful Job Interview

Job interviews call for you to present your very best self. Job interviews allow employers to judge you and how you will fit in with their organizations. You will be evaluated not only on your work experience and qualifications, but also on your manner, appearance, confidence, and enthusiasm. You may have a great resume, but if you do not interview effectively, you will not get the job.

Following are some of the common pitfalls or barriers that people run into when they are interviewing. Place a check mark in the check box next to the pitfalls that you struggle with.

- ☐ Effectively presenting my skills to the interviewer
- ☐ Maintaining eye contact
- ☐ Arriving on time
- ☐ Dressing appropriately
- ☐ Listening to the interviewer without interrupting
- ☐ Providing examples of my experiences
- ☐ Greeting the interviewer properly
- ☐ Asking questions about the organization
- ☐ Demonstrating knowledge of products or services

- ☐ Organizing my thoughts before speaking
- ☐ Remaining calm throughout interview
- ☐ Using the name of interviewer occasionally
- ☐ Exhibiting a positive, enthusiastic attitude
- ☐ Using correct grammar and pronunciation
- ☐ Closing the interview
- ☐ Following up

The following sections provide some basic, practical advice for succeeding in your next job interview. However, there are many excellent, in-depth resources for those who need more assistance. Some good places to look include:

- *Next-Day Job Interview*, Michael Farr
- *The Career Coward's Guide to Interviewing*, Katy Piotrowski
- *Interview Magic*, Susan Britton Whitcomb

Before the Interview

Proper preparation for an interview starts long before the interview itself. Preparing for an interview is critical. The following exercises can help you prepare for your next interview.

Review Your Strengths and Your Accomplishments   Analyze your strengths and weaknesses, your skills and experience, your interests and values, and your personal aspirations:

1. What are your strengths? _____

   _____

   _____

2. What are your weaknesses? _____

   _____

   _____

3. What do you value most in your work? _____

   _____

   _____

4. What are your career aspirations? _____

   _____

   _____

Research the Organization   Study your prospective employers. Learn as much as you can about their policies, philosophies, products, and services. Look up the company on the Internet. Talk with people who work there. Read over any material they publish (such as brochures or press releases). Use this information to answer the following:

1. What products or services does the employer provide? _____

   _____

   _____

2. What are the employer's goals? _____

   _____

   _____

3. What challenges does the employer face? _____

_____

_____

4. How can you help the employer meet these goals and face those challenges?

_____

_____

Review Anticipated Questions   The questions you will be asked during an interview will take many forms, and there is no way to have a response ready for every one. You *can* prepare answers for some of the more common questions. Following is a list to get you started. Feel free to write out answers to these questions on a separate sheet of paper or to practice answering them with a friend or family member.

1. What are your short- and long-range goals?

2. What do you see yourself doing five years from now?

3. Why do you want to work for our company?

4. What do you consider to be your greatest strengths?

5. What are your weaknesses?

6. How would you describe yourself?

7. Why should I hire you?

8. What are your qualifications?

9. How do you determine or evaluate success?

10. What do you think it takes to be successful in a company like ours?

11. In what ways do you think you can make a contribution to our company?

12. If you were hiring someone for this position, what qualities would you look for?

13. How do you work under pressure?

14. What have you learned from your mistakes?

15. Are you willing to relocate?

16. Are you willing to travel?

Prepare Questions for the Interviewer   Interviewers will expect you to ask thoughtful questions about the job and the organization. Never ask a question that is answered in the materials supplied by the employer. List several questions you might ask an employer.

_____

_____

_____

_____

Prepare What You Will Wear   Because the first few seconds of the interview are crucial, you will need to look your best. In most cases you should dress professionally and wear conservative colors. Even if the job requires you to wear jeans or a uniform, wearing nice clothes to the interview can't hurt. In addition, you should pay careful attention to your grooming. The following checklist will help ensure that you project a professional image before your next interview.

☐ Clean and press clothes.

☐ Shine shoes.

☐ Brush teeth.

☐ Apply makeup.

☐ Apply deodorant.

☐ Cover tattoos, if possible.

☐ Keep jewelry to a minimum.

☐ Brush or style hair.

☐ Clean and trim fingernails.

☐ Pack breath mints—just in case.

During the Interview

Most interviews last anywhere from 30 minutes to an hour. To make the most of that time, you need to make a good first impression and take every opportunity to emphasize the skills and experience you have that make you the best person for the job. The following tips can help you ace your next interview.

- **Arrive early.** Try to arrive 10 to 15 minutes prior to the interview.

- **Greet the interviewer.** Greet the interviewer by his or her last name (i.e., "Mr. Jones" or "Ms. Smith"). Never address the interviewer by using a first name unless specifically asked to do so.

> An individual who is convinced he or she is the best candidate for a job will have the best chance of convincing the interviewer the same thing.

- **Emphasize your strengths.** Use proof-by-example to illustrate your skills. For example, instead of simply saying, "I am an excellent salesperson," instead say, "When I was working in the marketing department, I helped increase sales by 40 percent …"

- **Ask questions.** When appropriate, ask meaningful questions, particularly if you're not clear about the details of the job. Never ask about salary until you have been offered a job.

- **Be enthusiastic.** Employers want to hire people who are excited about the work. You must project an air of confidence and enthusiasm about the interviewer's company and products.

- **Conclude appropriately.** Always thank the interviewer for his or her time. Close with a statement that sets the stage for appropriate follow-up activities such as, "I would really enjoy working for your company. May I call you on Thursday to see if a decision has been made?"

◼◻◻ Tell Me About a Time When You . . .

Most interviewers will want you to provide specific examples of your past successes. These examples, or stories, show the skills that you have used to solve problems and give employers a better sense of how you will behave on the job. Thus, an interview is a chance for you to tell stories about your accomplishments, providing details whenever possible.

Respond to the following three, common interview prompts by relating a story about when you handled the situation being presented.

1. Tell me about a time when you set a goal and were able to meet or achieve it:

_____

_____

_____

2. Tell me about a time when you had a problem with a customer or coworker and what you did to solve that problem:

_____

_____

_____

3. Tell me about a time when you took the initiative and became a leader:

_____

_____

_____

After the Interview

Persistence is key when it comes to getting the job you want. That means following up after the interview is over. Be sure to send a thank-you note expressing your appreciation for the interviewing opportunity. Use your letter as an opportunity to reiterate your skills and your interest in the position. Use the sample thank-you note that follows as a general guide.

> Even if you aren't interested in the position, send a thank-you note anyway. After all, they may have a position you *are* interested in later, and you want to leave a good impression.

November 16, 2016

Judy Smith
Employee Relations Manager
XYZ Corporation
Lexington, KY 26757

Dear Ms. Smith:

Thank you for taking the time to interview me. The position you described sounded extremely interesting and challenging.

I believe that my experiences as a secretary with Coldwell Banker and as an office manager with the Nationwide Insurance Agency would allow me to make a significant contribution to XYZ. My organizational skills and ability to meet deadlines make me an ideal candidate for this position.

If you need any further information or would like to meet again, please feel free to contact me at (606) 555-4567. I will contact you next week to discuss the next step in the selection process. Thank you again for your time.

Sincerely,

Sharon Thomas

Sharon Thomas

After sufficient time has elapsed following your interview, feel free to call the interviewer to restate your interest in the job. Don't be pushy, but let him or her know that you will do whatever it takes to succeed in the organization if they give you the opportunity.

> When it comes to thank-you notes, an email on the day you interviewed works well when followed up by a more formal letter arriving one or two days later.

When it comes to interviews, attitude is everything. It's normal to feel stress and anxiety. However, the better prepared you are for the interview, the less anxiety you will feel. Remember that most of the barriers you face can be overcome with planning, preparation, and a positive attitude.

Assessing Job Offers

Once employers have begun making offers to you, it is time to assess those job offers. Following are some of the questions you can think about when you receive job offers:

- Is the job a good match for you?

- Will the job provide you with the growth you will need to meet your long-term career goals?

- Are there opportunities for advancement?

- Are there opportunities to gain additional training and/or education?

- Are there positive fringe benefits?

- Is the salary in line with your skills and experience?

When you are preparing to accept a job, take your time to thoroughly evaluate the offer. If your answer to any of these questions is *no*, accepting the position might be a mistake. If you are unemployed and simply need to find a job to fulfill your most basic needs, by all means accept the job. While working at your new job, maybe other opportunities inside or outside the organization will become available to you.

However, if you believe that the job will make you miserable and you have other options, you may want to consider making a counter offer or negotiating for additional benefits. Either way, you need to consider how taking the job will enhance or detract from your career development.

Summary

Most people dread the job search. But job search knowledge barriers are often the easiest to overcome. Though it requires a lot of time and energy, anyone can conduct a successful job search. Just be sure to follow all of the steps in the job-search process and use all resources at your disposal. Don't get discouraged. Nothing can stop you if you are determined to succeed.

■■◻ Barrier Breakers

Aisha worked for about six years as a clerk for a restaurant distribution company. As the company struggled, her own work hours were cut in half. Aisha thought that this would be the perfect time to begin looking for a more secure job. The problem was that she hadn't looked for a job in ages.

A few hours at her local library and a visit to her local employment agency alleviated some of her fears. With a well-crafted resume, she was ready to get started. However, a mass-mailing and Internet-posting campaign yielded little results.

After asking her family and friends for networking contacts, she met James, her brother's lawyer. It turned out he was looking for a clerk to help him organize his office. Aisha's brother passed along her resume and she got an interview. Her brother helped her practice answering interview questions, and she learned as much as she could about the work of a clerk in a law office.

The interview went great, and Aisha landed the job. All total her job search took about four weeks, but it was ultimately just a question of knowing somebody who knew somebody.

That and being able to convince that somebody that she was the best person for the job.

PART 5

Education and Training Barriers

New occupations are created nearly every day. Most of the new and best jobs require workers to learn new skills. This often means getting additional education and training.

To take advantage of the opportunities in today's workplace, you must become a lifelong learner. That means you need to be prepared to turn every experience into an opportunity to build knowledge, skills, and wisdom. Being a lifelong learner can help you find a new job or keep your current one. More importantly, it can help prepare you for new career opportunities in the future.

The First Step: A High School Education

A high school diploma or its equivalent is a *minimum* requirement for nearly every job. If you never completed high school, you should look into completing your General Educational Development test (GED). Passing the GED certifies that you have the equivalent of a high school education.

You will have to prepare for the GED. Libraries, colleges, and local high schools often offer adult education courses designed to get people ready for the exam. For more information about the GED, call the American Council on Education (202-939-9490) or visit http://gedtestingservice.com.

The Value of Additional Education

Getting—and keeping—the job you want means having the skills and training to *do* that job. While most employers offer some form of on-the-job training, they will also expect you to come in to work with certain skills.

The better educated you are, the more valuable you are to an employer. Being successful—whether finding a job or on the job—may require you to go back to school and get additional education or formal training to enhance your skills.

Statistics show the value of education. College graduates earn, on average, almost twice as much over their lifetimes as workers with only high school diplomas. Following are the average weekly earnings for American workers based on the amount of education they have attained, according to the Bureau of Labor Statistics in 2014:

Education Level	Unemployment Rate	Weekly Earnings
Less than High School Diploma	11.0%	$472
High School Diploma	7.5%	$651
Some College, No Degree	7.0%	$727
Associate Degree	5.4%	$777
Bachelor's Degree	4.0%	$1,108
Master's Degree	3.4%	$1,329
Doctoral Degree	2.2%	$1,623

Also, any form of postsecondary education expands your job options. More education equals more career choices. In fact, the percentage of new jobs that require higher education is growing. Approximately 62% of all new jobs will require an associate degree or higher. In addition, workers with some form of postsecondary education and training are less likely to lose their jobs. More education represents more job security.

You can expect to pay thousands of dollars for a college education. The long-term rewards need to be evaluated in relation to the short-term costs of time and money.

Of course, everyone has his or her own reasons for continuing his or her education. List the reasons you might go back to school and further your education, as well as the reasons you haven't done so. The second column represents barriers you have to furthering your education—barriers that you will need to overcome.

Why I Need to Further My Education

_____

_____

_____

_____

_____

_____

Why I Haven't Done It Yet

_____

_____

_____

_____

_____

_____

Choosing the Best Educational Program

There are many ways to get additional training and education. You could go back to school in your spare time. Depending on your career goals, there might be training programs lasting months or even weeks to help you reach those goals. You could take evening courses or get your degree online. You could also get informal training by observing—or "shadowing"—workers in jobs of interest or doing volunteer work in that field.

Like all parts of your career, your education requires careful planning. That means choosing the right program for you. It is important to choose a program that matches your interests and helps you achieve your occupational goals. Complete the following questions to help you choose a program that is compatible with your goals (go back to Part 3 if you have trouble answering some of these questions):

- What are your career goals? _____

_____

_____

- What job would you like to work, provided you had the right education and training for it?

_____

_____

- What kind of degree or training program would you need to qualify for this job?

_____

_____

- Do you want to attend classes on a school campus, take courses online, or a combination?

_____

_____

- What schools offer the training or educational programs that meet your requirements?

_____

_____

- How much time and money can you commit to your education? _____

  _____

  _____

- What steps would you need to take now in order to enroll in the program that interests you?

  _____

  _____

There are well over 4,000 colleges in the United States, and that doesn't include the more specialized training programs. Some of the types of educational programs available to you include the following:

- **Traditional college programs:** Degree-granting programs typically require many hours of study and practice. An associate degree generally requires two years of *full-time* study at a college or university. A bachelor's degree generally requires four years of full-time study. A master's degree generally requires two years of full-time study *after* earning a bachelor's degree.

- **Alternative college programs:** Most people believe that to get college credits you must go to college and take courses full-time, during the day. That's simply not true. There are a variety of alternative programs designed to meet the needs of adults who are returning to school. Many colleges now offer distance-learning programs where you can complete courses online. Many colleges also offer weekend courses available to the public. Correspondence or home-study courses are available for self-motivated learners. The College Level Examination Program (CLEP) programs exist to give people credit for knowledge learned in a variety of nontraditional ways. Be sure to research all of your options.

- **Non-degree programs:** There are many quality private trade and technical schools that offer excellent sources of training. Many of these programs are in trade areas such as auto mechanics, cosmetology, nurse's aide programs, drafting, electronics, and heating and air conditioning repair. Your local high school or college may also offer continuing education courses in specialized areas. In addition, many community colleges offer noncredit courses at a very low price. Most of these programs require two years or less to complete.

Online Learning or Not?

Many educational programs have now been adapted to an online environment. These programs rely on wikis, blogs, email, web-supported textbooks, videos, social networking, and discussion boards to supplement learning. The following, quick assessment is designed to determine how comfortable you would be using this type of teaching-learning format. For each of the items, decide if the statement describes you or not. If it *does*, place a check mark in the check box in the **True** column. If it does *not*, place a check mark in the check box in the **False** column.

In school, I ...	True	False
like interacting with others through technology.	☐ 2	☐ 1
don't need to see demonstrations to learn.	☐ 2	☐ 1
make friends and maintain relationships through technology	☐ 2	☐ 1
am motivated to learn on my own	☐ 2	☐ 1
am comfortable learning using various technology.	☐ 2	☐ 1
can learn by discussing things via technology.	☐ 2	☐ 1
am comfortable communicating via technology.	☐ 2	☐ 1

Add the scores next to the boxes you checked to get your Online Learner Total. Write that in the space below.

Online Learner Total = _____

You should get a score between 7 and 14 on this assessment. Scores from **12 to 14** are **high** and indicate that you would probably learn well in online educational programs. You would enjoy classes that are completely online or hybrid classes that include some online instruction. Scores from **10 to 11** are **average** and indicate that you would learn pretty well in online educational programs. Scores from **7 to 9** are **low** and indicate that you would probably not learn very well in online educational programs; you should consider other forms of instruction.

Education and training programs have a wide range of requirements for acceptance. Also be aware that programs vary considerably in the *quality* of the education and training you receive. Be sure to carefully research any program you are interested in. A good place to start is http://collegebound.net.

Following are some questions to ask and things to look for in a school or training program:

- How much does it cost? How much financial aid is available?

- How long will it take to complete my program?

- What are the requirements for enrollment?

- What jobs will this program open up for me?

- Where is it located? Is there public transportation nearby? Do they offer courses online?

- What services are available for students with disabilities?

Think about and research your education options carefully, and then look over your answers to the questions on pages 83–85. Based on your research, which education program seems right for you at this time?

▣▣▢ Connecting Education and Career

In Part 3 you explored your career options and identified specific jobs that interested you. For each of the clusters that interested you, review the education and training programs that match those clusters below and circle any you want to look into. These represent general fields—there are many ways you can further your education within each one. Remember that this is only a sample of the kinds of programs available to you.

Agriculture and Natural Resources: Forestry, soil science, wildlife technology, animal sciences, agriculture, botany, landscaping, horticulture, veterinary medicine, environmental science, geology, mining practices, animal obedience training, farm and ranch management

Architecture and Construction: Computer-aided drafting, mechanical drawing, bricklaying, mechanics, plumbing, surveying, carpentry, construction technology, masonry, industrial arts, blueprint/schematic reading

Arts, Audio, Video, Technology, and Communications: Drama, graphic design, photography, literature, marketing, print and broadcast journalism, humanities, languages, creative writing, fashion design, communications, floral arranging, painting, sculpting, advertising, graphic design

Business and Administration: Public relations, speech, marketing, retail management, business management, economics, finance, labor relations, office management, secretarial science, accounting, bookkeeping, personnel management

Education and Training: Early childhood development, elementary education, secondary education, physical education, library science, special education, vocational education, adult education, educational psychology

Finance and Insurance: Bookkeeping, accounting, money and banking, finance, insurance, real estate, real estate law, business law, record keeping, business computer applications, clerical/office practices

Government and Public Administration: Architectural history, criminal investigation, political science, government, history, statistics, geographic information systems, law enforcement

Health Science: Medicine, nursing, radiology, emergency medicine, dentistry, laboratory science, kinesiology, genetics, physical therapy, nutrition, EMT training, radiology

Hospitality, Tourism, and Recreation: Home economics, food service, hotel and motel management, cosmetology, dietetics, textiles and clothing, recreational administration, cooking, culinary arts, recreation

Human Services: Family studies, psychology, sociology, human development, social work, education, religious studies, counseling, career guidance, philosophy, child development

(continues)

Information Technology: Business machine repair, computer concepts, computer programming, computer science, database theory and design, electronics, computer repair, computer systems analysis, computer security, web design

Law and Public Safety: Criminology, law enforcement, fire sciences, political science, military science, physical education, criminal justice, law, paralegal studies, contract law

Manufacturing: Auto mechanics, auto-body repair, electronics, industrial arts, welding, industrial safety, locksmithing, optics, offset printing, hydraulics, machine operating, nuclear safety

Retail and Wholesale Sales and Service: Marketing, purchasing, business management, real estate, cashiering, merchandising, retailing, sales, public speaking, consumer behavior

Scientific Research, Engineering, and Mathematics: Astronomy, earth science, geology, archeology, biology, chemistry, radiology, meteorology, engineering, geography, industrial organization, economics

Transportation, Distribution, and Logistics: Airport safety, driver education, flight safety, industrial distribution, navigation, truck driving, shipping regulations, railroad safety, ship systems

Overcoming Barriers to Education and Training

Postsecondary education and training opportunities are considered the best gateways to highly skilled and high-paying jobs. Often, however, there are numerous barriers that prevent people from furthering their education and block their chances for career success. In the exercise that follows, insert check marks in the check boxes next to any barriers that may be keeping you from going back to school:

☐ I have trouble learning new things.

☐ I lack the money to go back to school.

☐ I lack basic math skills.

☐ I don't want to take out student loans.

☐ I don't know what type of major or degree program is best for me.

☐ I live in an area with no close schools.

☐ I lack the motivation needed to complete my education.

☐ I dropped out of school in the past.

☐ I cannot fit classes into my work schedule.

☐ I don't know how to apply to schools.

☐ I am in poor health.

☐ I am too old to go back to school.

☐ I am a poor writer.

☐ I can't juggle work, home, and school.

☐ I am not certain how more school will improve my life.

☐ I have a poor high school record.

☐ I don't know about financial aid options.

☐ I don't have long-term education goals.

☐ I lack basic skills in reading.

☐ I don't know how to support myself and/ or my family while in school.

☐ I think that school would be too hard.

☐ I lack basic computer skills.

☐ I don't know whom to talk with about furthering my education.

☐ I have a mental or physical disability.

☐ I lack study skills and/or test-taking skills.

Some of these are the same barriers people face in getting a job. Others are mainly a question of attitude. But all of these barriers can be overcome with proper planning, a solid support network, and the right attitude. The following sections address some of the more common barriers listed above and strategies for overcoming them.

Negative Beliefs and False Expectations

Like many other people thinking about returning to school, you are probably reluctant because of certain misconceptions. For example, you may believe that all college students have just graduated high school. This is simply not true. In fact, non-traditional students are the majority on college campuses today. According to the National Center for Education Statistics, 38% of all undergraduate students are over the age of 25. Following are some of the common myths and false beliefs people have about going back to school. Realizing that these are just myths may help you to get rid of your own negative expectations.

Myth: *College is only for young people.*

Reality: More and more people are returning to school to get more training. There are no age restrictions on who can get an education, provided they have the energy and resources to learn.

Myth: *I won't be able to keep up.*

Reality: In actuality, one-fourth of the students enrolled in college programs in the United States are 30 years old or older. These students often do better because they bring a wide variety of work and life experiences that they can apply to their learning.

Myth: *College is only for extremely intelligent people.*

Reality: Yes, some college students are extremely intelligent, but they are the exception rather than the rule. Most college students are of average intelligence. Don't let people say you're not smart enough.

Myth: *I can't afford to go back to school.*

Reality: There are billions of dollars in grants, scholarships, financial aid, and loans available for those who know where to look. You won't know unless you apply for these funds. You might also consider community colleges and online degree programs, which are less expensive.

> Mindpower, not manpower, will propel you in the workplace of the future. Fast learning and critical thinking are the keys to being productive in the twenty-first century.

> In May of 2007, 95-year-old Nola Ochs graduated with a bachelor's degree in History from Fort Hays State University. Ochs went on to earn her master's degree at age 98. You're never too old to go back to school.

Myth: *I did not do well in high school, so I can't go to college.*

Reality: Even though your grades may not have been great while you were in high school, the important thing is who you are now. Most colleges and training programs will judge you based on your current motivation, letters of recommendation, test scores, work experience, interests in the community, and enthusiasm.

Myth: *More education will not help my career.*

Reality: All of the research indicates that the more education you have, the more employable you will be and the more you will earn.

Myth: *I can't keep up with the new technology.*

Reality: Many adult students returning to the classroom feel anxious about new technologies. Remember that part of the reason you are returning to school is to learn new skills. That means taking classes to help you use new technology as well.

Funding the Cost of Education

Though it is almost always worth it in the long run, higher education can be expensive. The cost of furthering your education will vary, depending on several factors. For example:

- What type of educational program are you considering? Do you want to go to a vocational school, community college, or four-year college? Generally, the longer the program, the more expensive it is.

- Is the school public or private? Typically, private schools are more expensive.

- Is the school a traditional one or does it provide training and education to people at a distance? Studying from home or taking evening classes can allow you to work during the day.

You should think of your education as an investment. That means you may need to borrow money in order to go back to school. The following funding sources can help you further your education:

- **State and federal financial aid:** Visit http://fafsa.ed.gov to get information and to submit a free application for federal student aid.

- **Loans from friends and relatives:** Friends and family can loan you money to return to school. Just remember that borrowing money from friends and relatives can cause tension in your relationships.

- **Employer reimbursement:** Many employers have tuition-assistance programs for employees returning to school.

- **Scholarships/fellowships:** Undergraduate scholarships and graduate fellowships are forms of aid that help students pay for their education. However, unlike student loans, they do not have to be repaid. Thousand of scholarships and fellowships are awarded to students each year. You should review searchable scholarship databases such as http://scholarships.com or http://finaid.org/scholarships.

- **Military student aid:** Student financial aid resources are available for students pursuing careers in the military and for veterans and their dependents. For more information, you can consult http://military.com/education.

- **Bank loans:** Banks will loan you money to go back to school, but these loans must be paid back with interest.

Consider these additional strategies for overcoming financial barriers:

- Talk to a financial aid counselor at a school you are interested in and learn more about financial aid resources and student loans.

- Visit your state department of education's website for resources, or visit http://studentaid.ed.gov.

- Get help completing financial aid forms from financial aid counselors in college, high school guidance counselors, or student-personnel professionals in vocational schools.

- Consider apprenticeships or one- and two-year training programs that are often less expensive.

- Begin your college education at a junior college or a community college in your area.

- Find a way to effectively go to school and work around your job. If you work in the evenings, you might consider attending a traditional college or vocational program. If you work in the daytime, you might consider evening classes or a distance-learning program.

List some steps you can take to fund your education. This could include things such as, "Start putting money in an education savings account," or, "Apply for financial aid."

_____

_____

_____

Barriers to Learning

Do you feel like you lack the basic academic skills to succeed in college? Did you perform poorly in high school or even drop out? If so, remember that a lack of academic preparation is a barrier that can be overcome with hard work and practice. Study skills, test-taking skills, reading skills, and other learning skills can be practiced and improved.

Remember that most vocational schools, colleges, and universities have academic-success centers with people who can help you improve problem areas. If you have a learning disability, or feel that you might, colleges, universities, and vocational training schools will make accommodations for you.

Consider these additional strategies for overcoming academic barriers:

- If you're worried about being accepted to a program, remember that a poor high school academic record can be overcome by good scores on admissions tests, extra-curricular achievements, work experience, and strong personal references. Talk to admissions counselors about the requirements for being accepted and what you can do to increase your chances.

> Poor reading, writing, and math skills may be hurting your career as well. Continuing your education will improve these skills— and increase your chances for ongoing career success.

- You can learn to study more effectively and take tests better. Visit http://studytips.org for advice on how to be a better student.

- If you have struggled with learning in the past, you may have a learning disability. Most people with learning disabilities have average or above-average intelligence—they simply have deficits in the brain that prevent them from processing information. If you have a learning disability, there are resources available to help you. You can find information and resources at http://ldaamerica.org and http://ncld.org.

- If you are uncertain about your chances of success at a four-year college or university, consider starting your education at a junior or community college in your area that provides transfer credits to other academic programs.

- Some schools offer credit for life experience through the CLEP program. CLEP (College Level Examination Program) gives you the opportunity to receive college credit for what you already know by earning qualifying scores on any of 34 exams. For more information, visit http://clep.collegeboard.org.

List some steps you can take now to overcome your specific academic or learning barriers. This could include things such as, "Get professional help for a learning disability," or, "Enroll in one evening course at a local community college as a test."

_____

_____

_____

■■■□ Identifying Your Learning Style

If you are going to be successful in pursuing any type of educational opportunity, it is important to identify the way that you learn best, known as your *learning style*. This quick assessment can help you identify those characteristics that form your preferred style for learning things. You can then use this information to identify a training program that fits your specific learning style and become a better student.

(continues)

For each statement, indicate the point value that most reflects how each statement aligns to your learning preferences. **1** = Not like me, **2** = Rarely like me, **3** = Somewhat like me, **4** = Usually like me, and **5** = Very much like me. Determine which learning styles best align with your preferences by adding the values you placed next to each statement and placing the totals in the **Total Score** fields.

In school, I...	Value
prefer written assignments.	_____
always write down what I need to do.	_____
find that writing notes helps me remember what to do.	_____
find that written assignments are easier for me to complete.	_____
always make lists of things to do.	_____
like lectures written on the board.	_____
read and then take extensive notes.	_____
Written-Word Learner	**Total Score =** _____

In school, I...	Value
learn by doing.	_____
learn by manipulating objects	_____
find that the best way for me to learn is through "hands-on" activities.	_____
always want to be doing something.	_____
learn best through practice.	_____
am most successful doing activities.	_____
like assignments that require me to use my hands.	_____
Physical Learner	**Total Score =** _____

In school, I...	Value
learn by watching others.	_____
find that most people think I have a vivid imagination.	_____
learn by watching demonstrations.	_____
read directions several times before starting something.	_____
prefer to have someone show me how to do things.	_____
like to watch how something is done before trying it.	_____
enjoy reading how things are done.	_____
Visual Learner	**Total Score =** _____

(continues)

In school, I . . .	Value
remember directions that are told to me.	_____
like assignments that are verbal rather than written.	_____
am an excellent listener.	_____
like when the instructor reads directions.	_____
can easily repeat verbal instructions.	_____
do well on tests that are about things I heard.	_____
can easily remember what I hear.	_____
Auditory Learner	**Total Score =** _____

For each category, total score values **7 to 14** are **low**, total score values **15 to 21** are **moderate**, and scores **22 to 35** are **high**. Mark the score for each learning style below.

Written-Word Learner = _____ If you scored high on this scale, you probably learn best when you are able to write as part of the learning process. You would enjoy classes that present information displayed as words, have reading and writing assignments, and allow you to utilize technology—including the Internet—for research and writing reports.

Physical Learner = _____ If you scored high on this scale, you probably learn best when you are able to try things out and touch and manipulate objects. You would enjoy classes which include opportunities to move around, complete experiments, use your body to express thoughts, and use eye-hand coordination.

Visual Learner = _____ If you scored high on this scale, you probably learn best by seeing and when you are able to watch demonstrations of something being taught. You would enjoy classes in which you can watch demonstrations, complete readings, and see diagrams and symbols to better understand information.

Auditory Learner = _____ If you scored high on this scale, you probably learn best when you have verbal instructions about something being taught. You would enjoy classes which include oral exams, class discussions, speeches, and lectures delivered orally.

The Importance of Lifelong Learning

Lifelong learning is the idea that people need to embrace learning—regardless of age—as a way of improving life, relationships, and careers. People who are lifelong learners set education goals and take the necessary actions to reach those goals.

Lifelong learning not only helps you build on your skills, it also helps you grow as a person. It can increase your appreciation for culture and your capacity for knowledge. It also can lead to greater employment opportunities and more financial rewards.

The following are characteristics of lifelong learners. Insert a check mark in the check box next to each description that applies to you.

☐ I am interested in becoming more knowledgeable.

☐ I am interested in new technology.

☐ I believe that learning will greatly improve my life and my career.

☐ I believe that a person can learn things outside of school as well as in school.

☐ I believe that education is more than the process of going to school.

☐ I believe that education provides the tools to learn how to solve problems.

☐ I believe that education increases an appreciation for music, politics, and the arts.

☐ I believe that more education will increase my income.

☐ I set education goals that are specific and meaningful.

☐ I am able to focus my energy on the task at hand.

☐ I am able to visualize my future.

☐ I take personal responsibility to create the life I want.

To be a lifelong learner, you must be motivated to learn as *much* as you can about *all* that you can. You must be aware of your needs and the rewards that will satisfy your needs.

Answering the following questions will help you to understand the value of learning for you. It may also help you make your education plans.

- What types of things would you like to learn more about? _____

_____

_____

_____

- What would you like to learn how to *do*? _____

_____

_____

- How do you hope to contribute to the world? _____

_____

_____

_____

- What can you do to make yourself more employable? _____

_____

_____

_____

- How can you become a lifelong learner? _____

_____

_____

_____

Make an Education Plan

Now it's time for you develop your own education plan. By writing down your education goals, you will be more motivated to achieve them.

◼◼◻ My Education Action Plan

Think about your education goals. List those goals and then provide action statements that will help you to reach them. Remember to make your goals specific, attainable, and meaningful.

Long-Range Education Goal (within the next five years):

_____

Actions I will take to achieve this long-range goal:

1. _____

2. _____

3. _____

Medium-Range Education Goal (within the next year):

_____

(continues)

Actions I will take to achieve this medium-range goal:

1. _____

2. _____

3. _____

Short-Range Education Goal (within the next three months):

_____

Actions I will take to achieve this short-range goal:

1. _____

2. _____

3. _____

Summary

Going back to school can be a frightening proposition. In the vast majority of circumstances, the more education you attain, the more money you will make, the more marketable you will be, and the more self-sufficient you will be. There are many different educational programs available, and there are steps you can take to afford them. The key is finding the energy and motivation to upgrade your skills and expand your knowledge. While more education may not be necessary immediately, it will be at some point down the road. After all, education is the key to long-term career success.

■■□ Barrier Breakers

Stacey was working in an optometrist's office as a receptionist and assistant. She sold glasses, did all of the paperwork, answered the telephones, made appointments, took customer payments, and cleaned the office when she was not busy. Stacey, however, was not happy with her job. She knew she could do better. But she also knew that "doing better" would require going back to school.

She had heard about a program in business administration and management at a local community college, but Stacey was 45. It had been more than 25 years since she had been in a classroom. Not to mention she hadn't really saved for college. However, she made an appointment to talk to a counselor at the community college anyway. He assured her that with her previous work experience to draw on, she would be able to handle the courses. He also pointed her toward some financial resources, including a scholarship for continuing-education students that she could apply for.

So Stacey applied. She not only got into the program, she also got the scholarship. After three years of study (most of her classes were in the evening), she earned her associate degree. She now has a job as a manager of business operations for a local retail chain. However, she still isn't quite satisfied.

Now she wants to go get her bachelor's degree.

Conclusion: Developing a Plan for Success

Developing a comprehensive plan is important in overcoming your barriers to employment success. A plan can help you to see where you want to go and feel confident about getting there. The *Barriers to Employment Success Inventory (BESI)* is designed to help you identify your most critical barriers, break your barriers into long and short-term goals, and take action to overcome your barriers to employment success.

By completing the *Barriers to Employment Success Inventory*, you will not only have specific information related to your most significant obstacles, you will also have the opportunity to develop a barriers-to-employment success plan that details how you will work to overcome them.

Please remember that all job seekers experience one or more barriers to employment success. Although they can make finding a job more difficult, conquering them is not impossible. The secret to overcoming barriers to employment success is to keep working to reduce or eliminate these roadblocks, and never give up.